CONNACHT

THE TEAM THAT REFUSED TO DIE

To all those, from near and far, who nurtured the game of rugby on and off the field, so that it could be enjoyed by generations of people in Connacht.

John Fallon
Media West (Ireland)

Billy Stickland
Inpho Photography

ISBN: 978-0-9956075-0-7

CONTENTS

PROLOGUE

The weather was foul in Cork on Friday, 29 November 2002. It was cold, wet and gloomy and the atmosphere wasn't much better inside the Rochestown Park Hotel in Douglas where Connacht were preparing to take on Munster in the quarter-final of the Celtic League that evening.

Connacht had prepared as well as they could in the circumstances but there was little doubt in people's minds regarding the likely outcome a short distance away in Musgrave Park later that evening.

Munster and Connacht may have been competing in the same competition, but they had little else in common at that stage, just over half a dozen years since rugby officially went professional.

In development terms, Munster were close to the topping off ceremony. Not content with setting the benchmark in Ireland, the Red Army were leading the charge into Europe in this brave new world, filling up grounds all across the continent with their thousands of fanatical fans.

They had become a movement, a side with a rich tradition who had embraced the professional era with fervour, style and substance.

Connacht, on the other hand, were still at the foundation stage, mired in quicksand at every turn.

Nothing new there then. For the previous century and more they had always been the poor relation, outvoted and outplayed, but always inside the Irish rugby family. Until now, that is. Now they were facing being cast aside, forever.

The 'Connacht question' had been rumbling on for a few years since the game went professional after the 1995 World Cup in South Africa. Connacht were not included when the inaugural European competition was launched that autumn, with the IRFU sending Leinster, Munster and Ulster into the new 12 team competition.

A platform in Europe was found for Connacht the following year when the Challenge Cup was launched, where they took their place alongside 23 other teams as diverse as Toulon on the Côte d'Azur to Treorchy in the Rhondda Valley.

The 1999 World Cup debacle in France saw the IRFU embark on an expensive campaign of bringing Irish internationals back from clubs in England, as they tried to ensure that the shock elimination they endured at the hands of Argentina in Lens would never happen again.

This was bad news for Connacht. The IRFU had not yet mastered the art of turning professional sport into a money-making mechanism so they embarked on a slash and burn mission. There were other cuts planned but disbanding the Connacht professional team would be the biggest saving of all.

The move to get rid of Connacht came at a time when Don Crowley of Galwegians RFC was president of the IRFU. Some may have thought that forcing the change when the man in the top job hailed from the west would copper-fasten the move. Instead it backfired, and it was to prove to be the biggest mistake in the union's campaign to disband the western province.

Steph Nel, the coach from South Africa who was in his third season, felt betrayed by it all. Warren Gatland had offered Connacht a glimmer of hope a few years earlier, when his astute recruitment and good planning had taken them to a European quarter-final, suggesting that the new era might be different to the century which preceded it.

I had come on board as team manager in the summer of 2002 and by then Nel had assembled a decent, motivated side which went out and won their opening five games in the Celtic League, a run of wins which was not matched until the march to the 2016 Pro12 crown.

Three of those victories were by a point while another was a three-point success over Leinster in Donnybrook. There was a genuine belief in the camp that this was a side going places.

That wasn't long changing once the rumblings grew, hinting that these players mightn't have jobs in a few months. By the time the quarter-final against Munster came round, the mood was

> *For the previous century and more they had always been the poor relation, outvoted and outplayed, but always inside the Irish rugby family. Until now, that is.*

predominantly one of uncertainty and deflation.

Not that it was obvious for long periods that night in Musgrave Park as Connacht took on a Munster side containing nearly all the Irish pack, as well as the half-backs, Ronan O'Gara and Peter Stringer, in front of a crowd of 8,000 souls, clad almost entirely in red.

The floodlights failed after 13 minutes of the match and some of us in the Connacht dugout wished they would stay off; anything to give a stay of execution, create a diversion or a new talking point.

The Connacht players put in an exceptional display that night. It was 6-3 to Munster at the break and it took a contentious penalty try awarded by Nigel Owens to put distance between the sides after the hour mark.

Two late tries made it 33-3 to the home side, and Munster went on to beat Ulster by 32 points in the semi-final before lifting their first Celtic League crown with 20 points to spare against Neath at the Millennium Stadium.

My counterpart, Munster manager Jerry Holland, was sympathetic to our plight and so too were his colleagues. But they had other things to worry about – things like winning the Heineken Cup final. They had been pipped in two of three previous finals and knew they just needed to find an extra inch to get across the line.

We envied their success, their fan base, their talent pool, their tradition, their swagger, their limitless gear. You name it, they had it, we didn't. But, most of all, we envied the security they had as they planned a glorious future.

We faced a horrible journey back up the road to Galway and a deeply uncertain future. There was still a match or two to come in the Challenge Cup but there were tears shed that night in Cork because deep down, many genuine Connacht

people feared that they had witnessed the last serious match the province would play. That's how serious the situation had become.

There were tears shed too in May of 2016, when Connacht emphatically claimed the Pro12 title in Murrayfield, beating Leinster by double scores to lift their first trophy in their 131-year history – a prize earned while playing an exhilarating brand of rugby.

At least 10,000 Connacht supporters, with less than a week to prepare, had managed to make the journey to Edinburgh, inveigling their way into beds all across a city that was packed out due to the hosting of the Edinburgh marathon and two large conferences.

On and off the field Connacht were heralded as possessing the best structures, their academy setting the pace in nurturing talent.

Connacht, on their way to lifting that trophy, beat Munster twice, the first time they had recorded home and away wins over an Irish province in the same season. In March, five Connacht players were on the field at the finish as Ireland ran in a record nine tries against Italy for a 58-15 win in the Six Nations.

Munster only secured sixth place and a spot in the Champions Cup on the final day of the season after another campaign that was marked by falling attendances and further drifting away from the business end of competitions.

While Connacht were singled out for praise at the IRFU annual general meeting a few weeks later, Munster were in the firing line. Chief executive Philip Browne warned that the union could no longer be the 'lender of last resort', after it emerged that Munster, Heineken Cup winners in 2006 and 2008 and semi-finalists as recent as 2013 and 2014, were over €9 million in debt and were unlikely to be able to make their repayments.

So how, in such a short length of time, have the fortunes of these sides changed so much?

The Munster chronicle may be told separately, and who knows, the fortunes of these side can fluctuate at any time.

However, this is the story of how a team came back from the brink more than once, before setting off on a magical journey that defied not only the odds, but their own proud, but humble history.

This is the story of how a team came back from the brink more than once, before setting off on a magical journey that defied not only the odds, but their own proud, but humble history.

John Muldoon stretches during pre-season

CHAPTER ONE
_Pre-season

The manner in which Armand Vaquerin departed this earthly world was, by any stretch, fairly dramatic. He picked up a revolver in *'Le Cardiff'*, the bar he co-owned in Beziers, dared his fellow drinkers to a game of Russian roulette and, to get them started, took the first spin himself, put the gun to his head, pulled the trigger and promptly blew his brains out.

It was 12 July 1993, just nine years after the most decorated player in French club rugby had retired. He was 42 and it was a brutal end to a life marked by a high level of violence on the field, years of leading with the boot, or fist, or whatever was handiest.

Armand, a fearsome loosehead prop, was the only player to feature on each of the Beziers teams that won ten French championships between 1971 and 1984. He won 26 caps for France in that time, naming the pub in Beziers where he spent a heavy night of drinking before picking up the revolver, in honour of the battles he endured with the Welsh at the Arms Park.

He was born in Sévérac-le-Chateau, a small hilltop town in the Aveyron department in the Massif Central and every August a tournament is held in his memory.

The Challenge Vaquerin attracts teams from France, Italy, England, Scotland, Wales and Ireland and matches are played in towns such as Millau, Lacaune, Camarés and Saint-Affrique. Usually, there are four double-headers played over two weekends and most teams play just one match. They are all pre-season friendlies and there is no outright winner.

The local organisers pick up the tab for flights, food and accommodation for all the teams, so it is an attractive proposition for clubs who want a five-day camp in decent weather. Connacht returned to the event for the third year in a row to fine-tune their 2015-16 preparations.

They took on Castres in the second of three pre-season friendlies, with coach Pat Lam anxious for several workouts, given that there were only going to be two Pro12 games in September because of the World Cup.

'Our goal from early on in the year was to win it. We just wanted to keep it quiet. It originated in pre-season, we just knew things were different.'

"We went for three games, plus our own internal hit-out, to give as many guys as possible games. We want to have tough decisions to make when we go to select the team," he said.

Castres, almost relegated the previous campaign after winning the Top 14 the season before, won the game 19-5, with Rodney Ah You getting the Connacht try.

The previous week Connacht had their first run-out of the summer when they entertained Grenoble at the Sportsground. It was a useful outing with 27 players getting game time but the leaking of eight tries in a 52-19 defeat ensured some video nasties for review. Jack Carty, Ian Porter and Ben Marshall got the Connacht tries.

There were more encouraging signs in the final pre-season clash away to Munster at Thomond Park, where Kieran Marmion, battling for a place in the World Cup squad, crossed for two tries, with a Nepia Fox-Matamua effort and a penalty try securing a 28-12 win. It was a taste of things to come.

Connacht were working hard to perfect the 2-4-2 system which Lam saw as the key to success. Various formations have been tried by teams but Lam went for one which had a lock and a back rower on one wing, the other two back rowers on the other wing and a middle pod consisting of the remaining lock and the front row. It basically meant that when the ball went wide there was serious beef on the wings to stretch and damage the opposition. Rob Penney tried a version of it in Munster but it was resisted.

The lock in the middle is the key and that job was handed to Aly Muldowney, who was heading into his third season at the Sportsground. He reveled in the responsibility.

"Personally, I loved it. We used the system for two years and the fact is it just took us that long to get good at it. It was a work in progress in the second year and we just worked on it in pre-season, every day. For example we would have Finlay Bealham and me in the centre and by the start of that season I never had to look to pass to him because we all practised not looking

Aly Muldowney and John Muldoon

when we passed. There were a lot of balls going down in training but we worked on why the ball was going down and we perfected it. You just passed and knew the guy would be there. We worked on it over and over again. We trained as we played and we played as we trained, over and over again until it became second nature to us.

"Handling was easy for me from my basketball days. I had played quite a bit of basketball to a decent level growing up in England and that stood to me. Catching and passing I've always found quite easy. When I played for Exeter, I was very much like a battering ram. That was tough to play because you're just trying to get the ball and hit the gain-line every time, you weren't really passing. The passing side of our 2-4-2 system is quite easy because you just have to get into position quick and you very rarely had to carry," said Muldowney.

The third year in a coach's reign is often the most productive. In year one there is a bedding-in process, by the second season the coach has shaped the squad and by the third campaign they are often ready to peak. Connacht were ready to explode in August 2015.

Connacht players and management have always been realistic about pre-season targets. Of course, they want to aim high but never before did they set sail with the

Shane O'Leary

target of winning the league. But they did heading into the 2015-16 campaign, a remarkable target for a side which had never finished in the top half since the home and away system was introduced in 2003-04.

Unsurprisingly, they didn't go shouting it from the rooftops...

"Our goal from early on in the year was to win it. We just wanted to keep it quiet," said Muldowney. "It originated in pre-season, we just knew things were different.

"We wanted to win it but on the outside we told everyone we wanted top six. I think top six would have been a good achievement for us.

"The first year wasn't a very good year for anyone. The rugby wasn't good. There were mixed signals coming on what we wanted to achieve and what we had to do.

"In the second year, things started to come good. We changed our goals a bit in terms of how we wanted to be, physically and mentally. We started getting a lot more organised and Pat was a lot more approachable and open to our ideas. It got a bit better but we were still playing a lot of one-off rugby.

"But then it came to the third year when it was about moving the ball, passing the ball, moving the ball into

space. We had all the big details in place, we weren't concentrating much on the small details. We just got the small details right and worked hard on that. Training was very easy because everyone was accountable and knew exactly what they were doing. It showed in the season with how much better it got right up to the final.

"We always knew that we should do well when the World Cup was on, so we all expected that. We were ready."

Fionn Carr was one of the most experienced players in the Connacht changing room heading into the new season and with two spells with his native Leinster and two at the Sportsground under his belt, he had been through a fair few goal-setting sessions.

He said that the target of going outright for the Pro12 title evolved from a series of meetings rather than a fired-up session, while the feel-good factor from what was happening in training was fueling heightened levels of expectation.

"We probably had a couple of different times where we sat down. We had meetings when we were in France. The goals are reset and obviously coaches speak about certain things at certain times.

"But I wasn't surprised by the target of winning the league, not with the squad we had at the time. Different

13

lads have different opinions, but at the time when we went to those meetings, guys were quietly confident.

"There were a number of short-term goals which contributed to the long-term goal of winning the league.

"As the season got going, everyone seemed to step up their game because the battle for places was so competitive. It got to the stage where we were winning games with different teams, different lads playing in different positions, different combinations. It moved it to that next level.

"Guys were competing at such a high level and obviously we were doing what we desired on the pitch. We were going out and winning. You were going out and playing to the best of your ability. Even the academy guys, they all had fantastic games and a fantastic year. It drove it on," said Carr.

Pat Lam reflected the confidence which was in the camp after a summer of hard work, displaying a buoyant mood as the new campaign was about to kick off.

"We have come off a nine-week pre-season which has been pretty brutal. We have worked the boys hard. It all counts now in these games.

"A good start is very important, every game counts, all the points count. Last year was fantastic for the Guinness Pro12 – going into the last week there were

still ten teams with things to play for.

"In the first seven rounds we have five games at home, so it's crucial to get off to a good start and get the points.

"The selection for this team in my time here in Connacht has been one of the toughest. We put a real emphasis on the perceived second stringers and how they can close the gap.

"That has made the competition even better and everyone is looking over their shoulder, everyone is pushing each other hard.

"At Connacht we have to be a team and so to do that, it's about the sum of all the parts.

"There's two ways to react when someone is missing, you can throw your toys out or you can get on. It's all about being prepared and being organised," he said.

He had worked hard from the time he had arrived in the Sportsground in 2013 to integrate the academy players, and with Nigel Carolan's conveyor belt continuing to unearth gems, Lam knew this could be the key to success, given that he didn't have access to the resources enjoyed by most opponents.

"I always say if you're good enough you're old enough. There's been a good group that has come through this year.

"We've had the likes of Conor McKeon, Rory Parata, Peter Robb, James Connolly, Sean O'Brien and Shane Delahunt, they've been involved with us in pre-season.

"It's not just the training. They can build relationships with the guys who are already established here.

"We don't have as many internationals as the others, but the way we see it as a coaching group is that we just have players that haven't been capped yet.

"Part of our role is to help them in their development and their game so that they achieve their goal of being capped."

At the other end of the spectrum, a trickle was starting to make their way into the Irish side and Lam felt their international selection clearly identified the pathway for young players.

"There's some serious talent here, and Nathan White making it, Robbie Henshaw making it, Kieran Marmion and Rodney Ah You last year, it motivates the guys and shows them what can happen if they work hard.

"This pre-season has probably been the best since I've been here, because not only the understanding, but the relationships have all grown.

"The biggest thing that's made a difference this pre-season is that we have put a real focus on ownership. Two-thirds of the group of players have been with us since the beginning and relationships are strong.

"Before we would have said: 'this is what we want you to work on' but the growth of the team is such that the boys are now doing their own skills, and all we are there to do is facilitate it. That has been a massive shift for us.

"We have a more mature squad. Learning comes from playing and reviewing as a team and as an individual. Our group is stronger. I am confident that with the preparation we put together, the boys are bigger, stronger and faster," added Lam.

They were ready to rock like no other Connacht team.

Peter Robb

15

CHAPTER TWO
_The Early Years

Connacht were as ready as any of the other Irish provinces for the arrival of professionalism in 1995. They had done as much as Ulster, Leinster and Munster to prepare for the biggest change ever in the sport – in other words, they had done next to nothing.

Just about everybody in rugby knew that the sport was heading towards professionalism and that the last bastions of resistance were about to come tumbling down.

But the IRFU, like the other seven traditional heavyweight unions in the global game, were accustomed to change taking place at a slow pace and, more importantly, on their terms.

However, once Rupert Murdoch's News Corporation put US$550 million on the table for the SANZAR countries (South Africa, New Zealand and Australia) to set up a professional league, everything changed, almost overnight.

Connacht had held a few strategic meetings in the early 1990s to see how professionalism might impact on the sport and, no doubt, similar gatherings were happening around the country and elsewhere. But how can you plan for something where you have no idea what might be involved? Would it be a case of players getting paid for matches on Saturday and heading back to their regular jobs on Monday morning? Where would the money come from, how would it be sustained and what sort of competitions would they play in?

Bear in mind that the All-Ireland League had brought the club game to new heights in the early 1990s, with enormous crowds travelling around the country to games, fueled in turn by acres of newspaper coverage.

Some of the bigger clubs such as Cork Constitution and Garryowen had notions that it would be them, and not the provinces, who would go forth to compete in these new European competitions which were being talked about, the same way that the clubs of France and England were stepping forward.

Prior to the All-Ireland League, the rugby calendar was much simpler. Players would return in August to train with their clubs. Dates were specified when matches could be played, usually not before the start of September or after the end of May.

By September the clubs would start the endless list of friendlies, traipsing up and down the country to play other clubs, often in annual games or reciprocal home and away matches, playing for nothing but enjoyment and maybe some bragging rights. There would be lengthy speeches at the post-match dinner and plenty of food and drink.

Provincial leagues would also kick in early in the season, often serving as trials for the upcoming inter-pro games. Connacht, never having enough indigenous talent, would keep an eye on what was happening elsewhere, particularly if a promising player had some connection to the province. In that instance, an envoy would be dispatched to try lure him.

The game may have been amateur but money was finding its way into players' pockets. Car keys and jobs were also being handed to them.

Connacht might play the Defence Forces or a visiting side, often from the north of England or Scotland, in preparation for the inter-pros where they would play each of the provinces once, along with the Exiles if they were participating. They might win a game each season but it didn't stretch much beyond that and they never won the inter-pro series outright, sharing the crown in the 1955 and 1956 seasons being the closest they came to glory.

The inter-pros were also regarded as official trials for the Irish team in the weeks leading up to Christmas, and by January the Five Nations took over. All games were on Saturday afternoons, two at home and two away. So, early on a Saturday morning, trainloads would depart from Galway, Limerick, Cork, Belfast and elsewhere for Dublin and Lansdowne Road, breakfast on board, pints before the game, and dinner on the train home that night. In between, the game would be enjoyed and maybe a bit of business done with someone you would follow up with during the week.

Then it was back to club action, the junior and senior cups in the provinces adding a bit of bite to the friendly circuit and by May there would be a few barbecues, maybe a sevens competition, a clean up of the club and the whole thing would close down for the summer, to start again in August.

Former Connacht
and Ireland coach
Warren Gatland

A hierarchy existed in player recruitment. A good player with a junior club was quickly snapped up by the bigger clubs, with the likes of Galwegians and Corinthians ruling the roost in Connacht. In turn, a big club in Dublin might have no problem picking off one of their players with the lure of a good job. There was minimal movement of players between provincial sides, least of all the key performers.

There was never any great effort to spread the game in the provinces and Connacht was no exception. You either played the game or you didn't, those involved in running clubs were either former players or their families. Recruitment drives were unnecessary for players, officers or supporters.

Money wasn't really an issue. Each player and member paid a subscription, a bucket collection was taken up at some games and outlays, for the most part, were small. Some local sponsorship helped balance the books and some fundraising, along with assistance from the cash-rich IRFU, took care of development projects.

It was more or less the same at provincial level. There were enough players to go round and more than enough money to fund the games. It was just a great social and sporting outlet for a section of society, and their year revolved around it.

The All-Ireland League changed that environment and, indirectly, made Ireland more capable of dealing with professionalism. Suddenly, club games had a purpose. A winning mentality, so frowned upon before, was injected into the equation. The role of the coach took a new level of importance. Inevitably, money entered the arena as well with some clubs amassing – and subsequently blowing – big sums on gates receipts. The game may have been amateur but money was finding its way into players' pockets. Car keys and jobs were also being handed to them.

Many of the clubs went through a boom and bust period – some are still trying to pay off debts incurred in the 1990s – but those glory years of the AIL were to prove invaluable in helping rugby administrators deal with full-blown professionalism when it arrived.

Professionalism was difficult for players to adapt to, but it would have been even more arduous had the AIL not broken the ground.

It wasn't just players that the AIL developed. The domestic club game also paved the way for a raft of coaches to take up paid positions with clubs, provinces and national teams.

Eddie O'Sullivan was Connacht coach in 1995 when the game went professional, but the western province

Former Connacht and Ireland coach Eddie O'Sullivan at Crowley Park

remained amateur for what turned out to be his only campaign in charge. The Cork native and former Munster wing cut his coaching teeth with junior club Monivea in Co Galway, a short distance from where he settled with his family in Moylough, after taking a teaching post at Holy Rosary College in Mountbellew. He also worked as a rugby development officer with the Connacht branch of the IRFU and coached Blackrock College and Galwegians in the AIL, as well as being assistant coach to Connacht when George Hook was at the helm.

A dispute over the length of his contract led to him stepping down at the outset of the 1996-97 season and, after a stint in charge of the USA national side, he returned to the AIL with Buccaneers before becoming assistant coach to Warren Gatland with the Ireland national team.

Gatland had answered an SOS call from Connacht in 1996 to come in and take charge following their parting of ways with O'Sullivan, with the former All Black hooker flying from New Zealand to Sweden to link up with his new charges for a brief tour there.

He may have been parachuted in just as the season was starting, but Gatland was familiar with Connacht, having spent four seasons with Galwegians.

He was persuaded to join Galwegians as a player-coach and put his job as a PE teacher in New Zealand on hold following an All Blacks match against Connacht at the Sportsground in 1989.

Galwegians were keen to nab an All Black as they tried to get a foothold in the AIL and Gatland, then just 26, jumped at the chance, not having a clue what he was letting himself in for. He had come through a system at Hamilton Boys' High School and Waikato which paved a pathway to excellence. It wasn't quite as developed in Galway.

Joe Healy, a Galwegians stalwart who played for 12 years with Connacht and who is now a respected pundit with RTE Radio and Galway Bay FM, served as assistant coach to Gatland while also continuing to play, beginning a strong friendship which has continued over the years.

"It was archaic back then. I remember one of the first nights he came up training us in Galwegians and one of the lads said he would go in and get the ball. *The ball*, singular! Gatty is standing there with this sort of 'you got to be joking, mate' look about him. But before long he got a bag of balls and the next thing you knew you were dying to get to a training session because you were moving with the balls, and there were planned moves.

Scrum-half Conor McGuinness, now a member of the Connacht professional game board (PGB), gets the ball away against Northampton Saints in 1997

"The tour that he came on was Buck Shelford's tour. They played against Connacht and I loved that and I played against them. They brought the rolling maul to Connacht on that tour. That was the first time I saw the rolling maul. We were all saying: 'how does this work?' It was the first thing he introduced to our game. I remember going to places like St Mary's and blitzing them.

"There was no maul prior to that. You would stand up and take the ball. It was my first experience of having sequences of play that would be predetermined. We might have a lineout, and run it or kick it would be the approach. Gatty introduced moves where you run it and then you might come back and work a switch with the winger or the outside centre. As a forward you were picking your lines of running. He introduced that element of planning and forethought. The other thing about Gatty is that in the four years he was coaching us I don't remember him ever raising his voice once. He was just very quiet and didn't say a lot. He played with us for two or three seasons," said Healy.

Gatland and his wife Trudi immersed themselves in life in Galway and progress was made on and off the field by Galwegians RFC, but then tragedy struck when the couple's first child Shauna was born with spina bifida

Billy Mulcahy on the charge against Leinster in 1997

and was not expected to survive. The Gatlands cut short their Irish stay and returned to New Zealand where their daughter died at just four months old. Gatland has often spoken of the kindness of Galway people at that time.

"Here I was coaching Galwegians, a big season for them and they had invested a lot of money in getting me to Galway. But they just turned around and said: 'your family is all that matters, do what is best for them'. The reaction in Galway is something I shall never forget."

Many in Galwegians RFC kept in touch with the Gatlands after that but few expected that he would be back. Yet it took Gatland no time at all to decide to take charge of Connacht when he was offered the post just as the squad was heading on that pre-season tour to Sweden.

The inter-pros were still on the go but this was the first season that Connacht saw action in Europe, being sent forward by the IRFU to compete in the newly formed European Conference.

The years spent with Galwegians served Gatland well in his new role but it still took a season for an impact to be made.

Gatland realised that it was vital that he changed Connacht from being a representative team into a club side. He turned their lowly status in the pecking order in Ireland into a positive, instilling self-belief and a bit of a chip on the shoulder into players. He looked at history and drew on the utterances of English invader Oliver Cromwell, and had t-shirts printed for the players with 'To Hell or to Connacht' on them.

It was a bit ironic then that the big breakthrough should come in his second season in 1997 against English opposition, a star-studded Northampton Saints side – although notions at the time claiming Cromwell to be a Northampton man were a bit wide of the mark.

But Cromwell was a *Sasanach* and Gatland knew that taking on one of his phrases would be enough to get the blood boiling.

The Lions had just returned from their victorious tour to South Africa and Northampton had five of that squad on board – Matt Dawson, Nick Beal, Paul Grayson, Gregor Townsend and Tim Rodber, all ready for the European Conference campaign.

Only Beal and Townsend saw action off the bench in a re-fixed midweek match at the Sportsground, where Connacht stunned them 43-13. McGeehan rolled out Dawson, Beal and Townsend for the return match at Franklin's Gardens, but Connacht turned them over 20-15 to book a place in the quarter-finals.

Townsend, who has returned many times as a player and coach to the Sportsground, remembers the initial

Tuesday afternoon clash at the College Road venue.

"I think it was a classic trap game. On paper Northampton had a good team, plenty of internationals and Lions, the weather was good and we thought we would be alright. It was a step into the unknown for most of us, especially the English players, but we thought we would be ok.

"But Connacht weren't long in getting stuck into these English visitors, as they have done many a time, and we weren't just able to get back into it.

"Connacht were really good in those days in upsetting rhythm and playing with so much passion, and with Eric Elwood dictating matters at stand-off, you knew that if you were off your game then you were not going to win.

"We thought we would win back in Northampton. It was wetter but again Connacht were the better team.

"But I have learned many times over the years you can't underestimate Connacht, especially at the Sportsground. I remember coming back with Montpellier around 2004 and we were absolutely hammered. The crowd went wild with every big hit," said Townsend.

That 1997 campaign, Connacht's second in Europe, broke a lot of new ground. Their earlier 15-9 win away to Bordeaux-Bègles was the first competitive win on French soil by an Irish province, a feat which would have been achieved a week earlier in Nice but for a dodgy late try.

The run was brought to an end in Agen in the quarter-finals on a 40-27 scoreline, but the campaign showed what could be achieved with the right structures. While Connacht were competing in the second tier in Europe, there was a genuine belief that the gap between them and the other three provinces could close. Suddenly, the professional era offered great hope to the game in the west.

The exploits of Gatland, whose innovations at the Sportsground included the 13-man lineout he has since used several times since at international level, did not go unnoticed in Dublin and when Brian Ashton packed his bags early after one match in the 1998 Five Nations, the job of Irish coach was handed to the Kiwi.

Connacht turned to another Waikato man to take charge for the start of the 1998-99 season, but the lofty heights achieved under Gatland were not repeated in the two seasons in which Glenn Ross was at the helm.

The initial form was good in Europe. Three opening wins suggested a repeat run through to the knockout stages was on the cards, but the campaign fizzled out with three losses.

Off the field, Connacht were also trying to make

Junior Charlie tucks the ball under his arm and sets his sights on Northampton full-back Nick Beal in the 1997 Challenge Cup

Connacht's Graham Heaslip contests a lineout against Leinster in 1998

Connacht's Mervyn Murphy is tackled by Tyrone Howe and Jan Cunningham in 1999

strides to meet the demands of the professional game, but often it was an uphill battle.

Bernard Jackman arrived for the first of two stints with Connacht for the start of the 1997-98 season.

"I took a part-time contract, seven and a half thousand pounds retainer and then match fees. The match fees were good. It was 500 pounds plus maybe 500 pounds win bonus. There were five full-time players at the time. I know that Eric Elwood was full-time. I think Graham Heaslip, Jamie's brother, was full-time. Mick Finlay and I think Junior Charlie and Mark McConnell were the five. I think each province was given five full-time players to start off and Gatty brought in Junior and Mark McConnell from New Zealand.

"Most of us were based in Dublin. We used to do field training in Athlone and we had gym training programmes. We were all over the place but they were exciting times.

"We had a good year that year with Gatty. We beat Bordeaux-Bègles in the Challenge Cup and then we beat Northampton home and away. We picked up a load of win bonuses. Gatty created the 'To Hell or to Connacht' t-shirts and that created a bit of a chip on our shoulder and a bit of identity, which we probably lacked. It got through to us lads in Dublin. Some of the Dublin

lads had Connacht roots but some of us didn't, but now we were pretty much coming down there to fight a cause.

"Whereas then Glenn came in from a Super Rugby-type environment in New Zealand and tried to implement that type of game plan. For us, we probably didn't have the skill-set or the tactical nous to play it and we struggled badly. And we lost that kind of identity. Then we were fully professional but we weren't professional at all.

"It wasn't all Glenn Ross' fault. We weren't professional enough. There were a lot of wacky Wednesday nights out in Galway and that sort of thing. And training-wise, because we were full-time, we were probably over-training.

"I was still a hooker. At the start of the second season, Glenn tried to convert me to a back row. So I played back row against Munster in an inter-pro match. Munster had a good scrum and I think Anthony Foley was under the posts before I broke so that was the end of it. I went back to hooker. In actual fact, I signed for Sale Sharks to get away from Glenn Ross and then two months later, he signed for Sale Sharks. I had another year with him and then he got cut from Sale.

"He had come in to Connacht trying to follow on from

Gatty and that wasn't easy. Gatty had a pragmatic game plan and he focused more on getting the group united, working on getting people to buy into the vision. Then Glenn came in and it was more about the end product. We didn't have a good culture but he was trying to implement strategy. Maybe he was the right person at the wrong time."

Steph Nel from South Africa was recruited to take charge and he brought a fresh approach to Connacht at a time when talks were advancing about the creation of a new Celtic League, involving teams from Ireland, Wales and Scotland.

Nel was a passionate and fiery South African with strong beliefs, who recognised that structures needed to be massively improved if Connacht were to keep pace with the rapid development of the professional game.

He quickly began to understand the Irish psyche but would often become exasperated because so many people were singing from different hymn sheets.

But he was committed from the outset and wasn't shy about pushing out boundaries, fueled by a strong work ethic. Like Gatland, he bought into the history of the region and immersed himself with the locals, and his company was at its most enjoyable when he had his pipe in one hand and a glass of Sancerre in the other. He abhorred inequality and spoke engagingly about the injustices and changes which had occurred in his own country.

When he arrived in Galway his office was in the industrial estate at Liosbán, training sessions primarily took place on the main pitch at the Sportsground as the back pitch had not yet been redeveloped, while the gym sessions were in Galway City Gym. It was far from ideal, especially in the gym where professional players queued for equipment with housewives and retired men.

"It was something else," recalls former prop Peter Bracken. "There were auld lads in there chatting and having the craic and doing a few weights. They'd want to talk for hours with you. If you met them you'd end up talking for two hours doing feck all training. We used to have to go in there with the blinkers on and get the training done and chat away then afterwards.

"What I used to do is I'd go in a good 15 minutes beforehand and just chat with the auld bucks and get it out of the way. They were great auld characters but they were there for the social occasion rather than the training. I used to find it better to go in – and I'd enjoy chatting with them – get the chat out of the way and then they'd leave you alone."

Des Ryan and Susan Mitchell were the strength and conditioning coaches and Bracken said it was clear that they had Connacht players in better condition than most.

"I always trained hard and when I left Munster to go to Connacht what I found was that the lads there were lifting a lot heavier than their Munster counterparts. It surprised me. It was a good surprise because maybe they mightn't have been as good as technical rugby players, but they were improving what they could improve."

Michael Swift arrived from England the same summer as Nel for what was to turn out to be a 15-year stint playing for Connacht. Few have seen as many changes as the versatile back five player, who was born to Irish parents in west London.

"I came over, there was an agreement in place that I was signing for Galwegians, but there was a contract for Connacht as well. I arrived over and it was the year that Steph Nel became coach.

"I remember the first ever Connacht get together pre-season. Only about 12 people turned up. That was a professional team but there were only 12 people there. There was no gear and it was very ad hoc. To be fair to Steph he very quickly got everyone into shape and tried to make the best of a bad situation.

"Some players didn't turn up as the weeks progressed. It was almost an open invitation to guys to come and play. That would have been in July so it was a quick turnaround, the pre-season games started in August. It was a massive undertaking with limited resources. Every week would go by and there were some guys we wouldn't see again and other guys would get a contract. We had to get everyone together and form a team because then the season started. It wasn't as important because there were fewer games. There was no league, it was AIL and provincial.

"The first get together was in the Sportsground in the old stand. We used Galway City Gym for our weights but, looking back, we didn't even have a physio at

Prop Jimmy Screene refuels

Kitman Tom Newell in 2001

training. We had to go off to a physio if we needed treatment.

"It's a comedy when you look back. You would be given a gym session to do but it might take a bit longer because the general public would be using your equipment and you had to wait in turn. It just shows how far things have come.

"To be fair to Steph he got together a system, but the first few weeks were torture. He said he wanted to find out what sort of men we were. It was very South African bish-bosh. He didn't know what to expect and what players he had to work with. He had to filter out the driftwood. But he got the show on the road and we were up and running," said Swift.

Off the field there were developments. The Connacht branch had rented an upstairs office in Liosbán industrial estate. It wasn't ideal, there was an industrial cleaning unit downstairs, but there was a good restaurant across the road and sufficient space for the ever-increasing number of people working for Connacht.

Prior to that, the branch headquarters tended to be at whatever office the honorary treasurer or secretary was based, with meetings taking place in rugby clubs and hotels.

Now Connacht had a base and it was to get better in a few years when a new headquarters was developed at

Coach Steph Nel puffs on his pipe during a pre-season game with Leinster in 2001

the Sportsground.

Spearheading all of that was the province's first CEO, Gerry Kelly, who took charge in 1999. He was an inspired choice and served Connacht diligently through the province's most turbulent period until he retired in 2012.

During the amateur era the elected president was the person in charge but the advent of professionalism required full-time presence on the ground. Kelly, who took leave of absence from a teaching post in Garbally College in his native Ballinasloe, was an ideal candidate on a number of fronts, having been involved in rugby all his life. He was president in 1995 so knew how the system worked with all the various committees.

He had also been a selector and later team manager to the Irish schools side for several years and this was to prove hugely beneficial when it came to recruiting players for senior rugby.

When I joined as team manager in 2002 I was amazed by the workload Kelly had. My sole responsibility was the professional side but the demands of that meant most working days were 12 hours long.

But Kelly had all the other departments and grades to deal with. He might go from a meeting where we would sign a senior player to a meeting of the stadium committee, the re-grading committee, the schools committee or whatever next group came through the door. It was endless and all these committees, manned by volunteers full of good intention, expected the hired help and the top man to be present.

But Kelly knew how the system worked and ploughed along. The development of the new branch headquarters, which opened just after the start of the 2002-03 season, heralded the start of what we all thought would be start of a new era for Connacht rugby.

It was the start of a new era alright, just none of us envisaged how difficult it would be.

Coach Glen Ross in a teamtalk in 1998

John Muldoon takes
on the Dragons defence

CHAPTER THREE
_September 2015

Connacht defeated Newport Gwent Dragons 29-23 in their opening match and were fourth in the table after the first round. It would turn out to be the lowest position they would occupy all season.

They went into it with a good record against the Dragons, especially in the opening round.

This was the 28th meeting between the sides in the Pro12, and the three tries to two win was Connacht's 18th triumph over the Dragons.

It was the fourth time they met at the Sportsground on the opening day of the season, with Connacht coming out on top on each occasion.

The Rugby World Cup meant that there were just two games in September and captain John Muldoon warned of the need for a big start, given that five of their opening seven matches were at the Sportsground.

Muldoon said the need to chalk up the points early in the season to achieve their primary aim of European

Champions Cup was obvious, with most other clubs losing a greater number of players to World Cup duty.

Their drive to qualify for Europe's premier competition off their own steam for the first time was thwarted the previous season when they fell away and were then defeated by Gloucester in a thrilling play-off which went to extra-time.

"It was no consolation to be told you were in the match of the year when you come out on the losing end of it after 100 minutes.

"This season we want to be top six and it doesn't have to be sixth, that's what we're saying. Just get up there, stay in there.

"We managed to do it for a lot of last year but ultimately just fell short and were disappointed with the way we finished," Muldoon said.

The long-serving captain, heading into his 13th campaign, could see a lot of green shoots in the

Rory Parata and Andrew Browne in support as Nepia Fox-Matamua goes forward

Connacht camp and this added to the level of optimism.

"You look at some of the younger fellas coming in, they have a spring in their step. You're looking at the depth in positions and, when you can see these fellas knowing that they've got an opportunity and some of the older fellas, myself included, looking over their shoulder, then you know you're in a good spot.

"That's the way it's been for the last couple of weeks. There's been a good edge to training over the last couple of weeks," he added.

But Pat Lam warned that while they had a good record over the Dragons, winning all bar one of the previous 13 meetings at the Sportsground, little could be taken for granted against the Newport side.

"They have made a lot of signings. They have some big players in. Sarel Pretorious has come across from Super Rugby, he's a quality player.

"One thing about the Dragons is that you have to win the physical battle. Some of the games against them have been pretty close and they were won up front.

"They are certainly a strong side and we have to be on the money both mentally and physically.

"I'm confident that the preparation that we've put in has been superb. Looking at the boys, they are bigger, stronger and faster," said Lam.

A solid opening half display, which saw Nepia Fox-Matamua crown his debut with a try, pushed Connacht 14-3 in front at the break and while Pretorious marked his maiden voyage for Dragons with a try, Lam's men sealed the win after the break with Danie Poolman and Fionn Carr touching down to crown an encouraging start.

The win came at a price as replacement Eoin McKeon was ruled out for three weeks with a knee injury but Lam felt the manner in which they dealt with a rally by the Welsh was a sign of their growing maturity as a team.

"While we had our best finish in the league and achieved a lot of milestones last season, we were all extremely disappointed to fall just short of our ultimate goal.

"But getting so close has instilled real belief that we can achieve it this season and we are determined to do so.

"At the end of the day we'll take the four points from the Dragons game but certainly it's a very quiet changing room. We still got the right outcome and the outcome's important, but the process just wasn't spot on tonight," said Lam.

Try scorer Poolman, commencing his fourth season at the Sportsground, felt that the pain of coming so close to

Danie Poolman scores against Dragons in the opening round

Bundee Aki congratulates
Fionn Carr on his try
against Dragons

Champions Cup qualification a few months earlier had been turned into a positive.

"We learned a lot from that game against Gloucester last season. It showed us the way we can play and what we are capable of in attack.

"Obviously we were so close, and I think a lot of the guys are emotionally hurt by that. But then they took that defeat and we are now driving towards achieving that goal this year because we saw how close we got and how heart-breaking it was.

"During the whole pre-season everyone did really well. We grew a lot as a team, putting accountability on each other and expecting more from each other. We don't want to take a backwards step," said the South African.

A week later Connacht headed for Scotland bidding to end a seven-match losing run against Glasgow Warriors.

But the newly crowned champions were having none of it and looked to be out of sight when they raced into an interval lead of 23-6, which they extended by another seven points just after the break.

It looked like a damage limitation exercise from there for Connacht, but a try from John Cooney got them back in the game. A penalty try followed before Poolman got his second of the campaign and two points were secured when Fox-Matamua also crossed for the

second week in a row after 75 minutes.

It finished 33-32 to the champions, who had surrendered their 20-match unbeaten run at Scotstoun the previous week against Scarlets. It also ensured a win for Glasgow forwards' coach Dan McFarland against the side he had served as a player and coach for almost a decade and a half, before moving to Scotland during the summer.

"We always admired what he did with Connacht," said Warriors head coach Gregor Townsend. "We were looking for someone to come on board and work on our set-piece and we were delighted when he committed to us and he has settled in really well," said the former Scottish international.

Ben Marshall sustained a fractured arm which would leave him on the sidelines for six weeks, but it was interesting to hear what goals another lock, Ultan Dillane, had set himself for the season.

"Establishing myself as one of the senior second rows would be brilliant for this season," said the then 21-year old from Tralee.

"I am living with James Connolly and Eoghan Masterson. Masterson's success last season with Emerging Ireland – that would be an incredible achievement if I could get that this season. That's the

Bundee Aki celebrates against Dragons

Eoghan Masterson offloads against Glasgow Warriors at Scotstoun

Hooker Tom McCartney is collared by Glasgow defender Rob Harley

big one but I just want to establish myself now."

Five months later he made his senior Irish debut against England in the Six Nations.

Seven tries and six points had confidence levels soaring at the Sportsground but they had to wait three weeks for their next battle as the Rugby World Cup kicked off in London.

Robbie Henshaw and Nathan White were selected in the Irish squad for the tournament, with Kieran Marmion on standby, and the inclusion of the pair meant it was the first time since 1999 that Connacht had two players at the World Cup. Eric Elwood and Matt Mostyn were the pair from the province that featured back then.

Connacht's only other representative in the intervening years at the World Cup came in 2007 when Gavin Duffy was selected.

Connacht had a presence at the wonderful opening ceremony at Twickenham, with Pat Lam representing Samoa on the field as each of the 20 countries were introduced during the gala event prior to the tournament's opening fixture between England and Fiji.

There was a further Connacht connection to the opening day with John McKee, who served as forwards' coach under Steph Nel and Michael Bradley, in charge of the Fijians. Their backroom team also included physio Brian Downey, who had spent several years at the Sportsground.

Lam made a few sojourns to the Rugby World Cup for some corporate and media duties. Naturally this was as well as keeping an eye on his beloved Samoa, who he had represented three times at this tournament, and for whom his cousin Jack Lam was a key figure.

But as the tournament progressed it was the guy who was playing out-half for the United States who captured his attention.

And he became more and more interested as he discovered how a young player from Dublin, who was unable to break through in Leinster or Ireland, had headed for America to chance his luck there.

AJ MacGinty had gone to New York in 2012 to study and play some rugby before the former Blackrock College student got an opportunity to do a Master's degree at Life University in Atlanta.

By the time he had finished studying he was qualified to play for the United States and had progressed through the ranks with his adopted country, making his debut against Samoa in the summer of 2015. Suddenly, he was playing in a World Cup.

Within weeks of it finishing he was at his new base at the Sportsground in Galway and would go on to be a key figure in the Pro12 triumph.

THAT WAS CLOSE...
Captain John Muldoon reflects on what might have been against Warriors

CHAPTER FOUR
__Marching Season

The man who had led the fight to save Connacht stood halfway up the concrete staircase at the back of the West Stand in Murrayfield, trying to get a glimpse of the Connacht team bus arriving at the ground for the Pro12 final.

All around him on the staircase were dozens of Connacht fans, clad in green and white from head to toe, waving flags and singing and cheering. They were oblivious to the fact that if it wasn't for the man beside them wearing the Connacht scarf, there wouldn't have been any reason for any of them to be in Edinburgh that day.

Billy Glynn held on to his spot until he saw the team bus swing into view. The place went mad! Slowly, it inched its way forward, the decibel level rising all the time. The crowd surged forward and just as things began to calm down, Pat Lam emerged from the door of the bus and gave a big fist pump. The place erupted!

"I thought I'd never see the day," said Glynn, shaking his head as he moved off to find his seat. "I thought I'd never see the day, did you?" he asked. There was no need to answer.

It is, of course, unfair to imply that one man saved Connacht. The threat to disband the province in 2002-03 was prevented by the toil of many people, and to elevate Glynn on to a pedestal is not to undermine them.

But even his detractors, and it's safe to say there would be a few, would admit that he was the right man in the right place to lead the battle.

Strange then that on the biggest day in the province's history, Glynn was not on any VIP list. He bought his own match ticket, sorted out his flights and ate a pub lunch of fish and chips on his way to the match.

But Glynn is one of those people who really doesn't pay much heed to what people say or think of him. After all, you don't become a Revenue sheriff without having a fairly thick skin, given that you aren't always ringing a bell or knocking with your knuckles when you come to a door.

Tom Newell, my predecessor as team manager, had a great saying which was applicable to many things in

Connacht, and which coach Steph Nel regularly used: "It's not the size of the dog in the fight that matters, it's the size of the fight in the dog."

This was certainly applicable to Glynn, and he had plenty of bite to back up his bark.

I had a few rows with him when I was team manager. He was chairman of the management committee that oversaw the professional team, as well as being one of the Connacht representatives on the IRFU committee, so he was around the place a lot of the time.

I recall one particular day a few months after I came on board. We had enjoyed a great start to the season, winning our opening five games in the Celtic League. The players were flying fit after a great pre-season under the guidance of Des Ryan and Susan Mitchell, and wins over The Borders, Cardiff, Leinster, Newport and Bridgend had confidence levels soaring. The Leinster win, thanks to a late Mark McHugh drop goal in Donnybrook, was the highlight of the province's best ever start to a season.

The fear which Billy Glynn and the other Connacht officers had was that a decision to disband the professional team would be implemented and that it would be extremely difficult to reverse it.

Pontypridd took the long road to Galway and were a shambles by the time they arrived for our sixth match. Back then it was still customary for one of the host club to meet the opposition on arrival the day before a game and I had arranged to meet them and guide them to Crowley Park for their captain's run.

It was only the second season of the Celtic League and the travel back and forth across the Irish Sea was still testing for teams. In Connacht we were fortunate that Keller Travel in Ballinasloe organised the trips and it's testimony to the work of Pearse Keller and Michael Kelly that they are still doing it more than a decade and a half later.

Pontypridd, clearly, didn't have such good assistance for their trip to Galway for a Saturday afternoon kick-off. They crept from their beds in the valleys shortly after 3am on Friday morning, drove to Stansted Airport and then flew to Dublin. There was no motorway to Galway at that time and after hitting Friday traffic in every village and town along the way, they finally arrived at the Corrib

Great Southern Hotel several hours late on Friday evening. They were wrecked!

They cancelled their captain's run and instead just walked as far as Crowley Park and back. Things weren't much better for them the following morning, the day of the match. My counterpart in Ponty rang shortly after 9am to say that he had gone with their kickers, Neil Jenkins and Ceri Sweeney to the Sportsground, but their balls were flat and could I organise a pump?

That was duly sorted and when I arrived at the Radisson SAS Hotel for our pre-match meal I opted not to outline the difficulties our opponents were facing, although when Steph enquired what shape they were in, I just nodded and winked to suggest 'nothing to fear here'.

We were stuffed 40-0. The defeat would even have been bigger had they not had to wait half an hour to get their first score, even though they dominated from the start.

The mood was fairly sombre by the time we went back to the Radisson for the post-match meal. The hotel had come on board as a great sponsor and the general manager Mike de Haast, a passionate South African rugby man, was to prove to be a great friend of Connacht in the turbulent times ahead.

Pontypridd, perhaps still suffering from some sort of jet lag which, unfortunately, didn't seem to bother them during the match, got their times all wrong and didn't show for the meal until about two hours after the scheduled time.

As the clock ticked on I told our lads to go ahead and eat and head away. Billy Glynn took exception to this as he felt we should wait for our guests but I pointed out our players needed to get their recovery in place, not least as we were heading to France the following weekend, and that should take precedence.

Steph jumped in as well and there was a bit of a row, and most of our players were heading for home by the time Pontypridd showed up, dressed to the hilt for a night out in Galway.

Gerry Kelly, the chief executive, got wind of the row and felt there might be a follow-up and, sure enough, around 9am on Monday morning, Glynn came flying in the door of the branch office in the Sportsground and stopped at my door. "Well, young Fallon, how are we fixed this week, are we all set to go? Good." And on he went. He had said his piece on Saturday, he took no offence at what was hurled back at him, nothing was being taken to the grave. If he had something on his mind, you got to hear about it and he expected the same in return.

He had plenty on his mind as the 2002-03 season developed and the sounds coming from around the committee table in the inner sanctum of the IRFU did not make for good tidings for Connacht. Money was becoming scarce as they grappled with the demands of the professional game. Cost-cutting measures were being looked at and the idea of reducing the number of professional teams from four to three was gaining currency.

There was a lot of smoke and mirrors but Glynn had spent close on a half century involved in rugby at all levels at that stage and could see that the threat to cut Connacht was gaining momentum.

He could not have envisaged finding himself in such a position when he went through the gates of Garbally College in Ballinasloe in the mid-50s and shortly afterwards, encountered a rugby ball for the first time.

The son of a Tuam solicitor, Jimmy, his older brothers had gone to St Jarlath's College, the renowned Gaelic football nursery in the town, but for some reason it was decided to send the youngest boy, in a family of four sons and two daughters, to boarding school in Ballinasloe.

Glynn, like his father before him who was an Irish schoolboys champion in 1917, was keen on track and field, while some of the family played golf and one brother was a handy footballer.

"But I had never heard of rugby, I had never seen a rugby ball," said Glynn. "There was no television, so there was no way of seeing rugby. I will never forget my first introduction to rugby. I ran out in Garbally on my first day of school, you went in and got your desk and books and you had the rest of the day off. Everyone then got togged out and ran out and got allocated to pitches. I ran out on the junior pitch and a fella had a ball and he kicked it and I went to get it and it hopped away from me. Then I realised it was a different shape and that was my introduction."

It was the start of a rugby career which saw him play for Galwegians, UCD and Connacht, before going down the officer route with 'Wegians and the province, culminating in his election as president of the IRFU in 2012.

But nothing, in all of that time, occupied him as much as saving Connacht in the winter of 2002-03.

"In the 1980s I came in as chairman of selectors for the Connacht team. I was a selector first and then I took over as chairman of selectors.

"They needed people to fill it. There was no great interview. It wasn't that difficult and you were also available to travel around the country at weekends. Most

Connacht stalwart Billy Glynn

of our players came from outside Connacht and you'd hear about some fella who had a connection to the province and you'd go and watch him. You'd track the guy for the whole match and it was very interesting. You would learn an awful lot from it. Then I took over as chairman when John Callanan retired. Chairman was really the manager in the amateur days, you had to look after everything, but it was a very interesting job.

"Then in the mid-90s the game went professional, that's when things started to change.

"One of my jobs as manager was to get players to sign up to full-time contracts. At that stage we had five full-time contracts, we had about 13 part-time contracts. And that was it. We had a couple of amateurs with a fee per game. The full-time contract was £10-15,000, part-time was probably £5,000. I remember the match fee was £350 and there was a win bonus.

"We trained in Tullamore RFC, once or twice a week. We would train up there and most of the lads would be coming from Dublin, a couple from Limerick and from the west. I remember well going to Tullamore."

The progress made under Warren Gatland looked like being repeated in Steph Nel's third season but the five-match winning start gave way to uncertainty about the province's future and before long events off the field

were dominating the headlines, much more than what was on the pitch.

It would have helped, of course, had there been a line of communication clarifying what was being considered at IRFU level. But the information was coming in dribs and drabs, a leak to a newspaper, a comment at a meeting, or a player in another province passing on word of something he had heard.

As Christmas 2002 approached there was scarcely a day passed without a player knocking on my door looking for reassurance on something, while next door chief executive Gerry Kelly was fielding queries from all quarters.

Our lack of information to the players could have been interpreted as evasiveness but the reality was that we were no wiser. It was a deeply unsettling time. We had made a lot of progress that season, putting structures in place for a professional sporting environment and it was all being undermined by shenanigans which seemed a million miles away from elite sport.

The fear which Billy Glynn and the other Connacht officers had was that a decision to disband the professional team would be implemented and that it would be extremely difficult to reverse it.

The fear levels grew in January 2003 and a campaign

to oppose the idea started to gain some momentum. Support was sought from politicians, a media campaign was intensified, while support from all over the province, including other sports, began to emerge.

Getting all the Connacht clubs, especially the junior ones, on board was also important. A lot of clubs had felt left out when the professional era came in and with some quarters in Dublin suggesting there might be a windfall for these clubs if money was not being spent on a professional team in the west, it was important to have a unified stance.

Crowds were growing at Connacht games but they were still very small. The first test of what level of support was present on the ground came when a public meeting was called to discuss the situation.

Steph Nel was horrified by the unfolding crisis and wanted to distance the players from it as much as possible. We still had a European campaign to fulfill and the changing room was filled with chatter about what was happening with their jobs.

It was decided to keep the players and management away from the public meeting, so I was dispatched to represent them. The meeting was arranged for the Radisson SAS Hotel and the likes of Ralph O'Gorman of Galway Bay FM and auctioneer Danno Heaslip, a former

Connacht and Galwegians scrum-half, were among the organisers.

Mike de Haast in the Radisson also rallied the troops. We used to hold team meetings in a section known as the Backstage Bar and it was presumed that this facility, which might hold a hundred or two, would be sufficient.

But de Haast could see which way the wind was blowing and he switched it to a large ballroom with hundreds of seats. I remember sitting near the top, facing the stage, and there were about a dozen or two people around. I had been asked to speak at the outset and while I could hear more people shuffling in behind me, I was dumb-struck when I stood up and turned around. There were hundreds of people there, not just in the seats but up along the sides, more than you would see at a lot of Connacht games. I can't recall what I said in my few words to them but you could sense they were fairly animated and that kept increasing with each speaker. By the time Joe Connolly, the former Galway All-Ireland winning hurling captain, stood up and launched into an awesome speech about preserving identity and the need for equality, it was clear the crowd were ready for a battle. Many of them had no direct involvement in rugby but, for some reason, they felt this would be as good a cause as any to adopt after decades

of feeling downtrodden.

A movement had started and before long petitions were being organised, support was being sought from all quarters and plans were being made for a march on the IRFU headquarters.

The potential disbandment of Connacht and the mounting opposition to such a threat began getting increased media coverage, something which did not sit well with a lot of IRFU people who were accustomed to carrying out their business behind closed doors.

It didn't help matters either when a minority of the opposition became personal in their stance and some banners had to be removed at a Challenge Cup game against Pontypridd at Dubarry Park in Athlone, an incident which only served to widen the chasm.

A key factor, though, was that Connacht chief executive Gerry Kelly and his counterpart in the IRFU, Philip Browne, maintained lines of communication throughout the whole saga. It was a vital link, not least as there was no shortage of brickbats flying around in the media and in meetings.

The IRFU stance was that cost-cutting measures had to be examined. The increased demands of professionalism resulted in a forecasted loss of €4m for the union that year, projected to rise to €7m the following year.

They maintained that disbanding the Connacht team was just one of the measures being considered and as recent as September 2016 Philip Browne, asked to comment on a number of items for this book, stressed that they had never decided to disband the side.

"Like many urban legends the suggestion that the IRFU had decided to disband Connacht Rugby is one that continues to persist – but is simply untrue.

"The 'legend' was created out of an emotional reaction by some to one of the difficult questions that the IRFU reviews almost every year – How do we sustain our professional game model in face of two finite resources – money and players?

"This is a normal business function – looking at the business and the risks attached. The IRFU has always operated in a challenging environment and as such the mantra that 'we must all live within our means', pre-dates professionalism. Rugby has always had to operate within the reality that we work with two finite resources – players and finance.

"Every union committee discusses the financial and business environment we operate in. These discussions, as distinct from decisions, usually remain within the union committee. However, one discussion on the future of the game resulted in an incorrect assumption by some that the IRFU had decided to disband Connacht Rugby. The IRFU has never taken a decision to disband Connacht Rugby," said Browne.

But, of course, that is what the battle was about in 2002-03. Connacht, with just two representatives on the 22-man committee, just couldn't afford to let it go to a vote. They would be defeated. "And there would be no way back," said Glynn. "We would be gone and gone forever. Look at what has happened to other teams who have disappeared. None of them ever came back and we wouldn't either.

"The IRFU had cash of about £22m when the game went professional but after several years of paying players and bringing them home from England, that was beginning to get well shot.

"The attendances were small everywhere. You may get 3,000 at Thomond Park but it hadn't really clicked in at that stage. The Ulster victory in Europe helped that. But what made the difference was the Heineken Cup final in 2000 and Munster getting narrowly beaten by Northampton. Pat Lam captained Northampton that day and that win by them, funnily, had a knock-on benefit for Connacht and the other Irish sides. Ronan O'Gara and that kick he missed got Munster moving and that started to lift everything. Their near misses created a huge following and in time we all benefited from the surge in interest. We just needed to hang in there and get our chance.

"But we were having terrible difficulty contracting players because we couldn't offer them anything other than one year. The other provinces could offer great security. We couldn't do that to anybody and that was screwing us. We could only get players who were from Connacht and those who weren't wanted elsewhere," added Glynn.

Around 2,000 people – more than attended a lot of Connacht games – marched through Dublin to the IRFU offices on Lansdowne Road to hand in a petition calling for the threat to be discontinued and for Connacht to be treated equally as one of four Irish provinces in the professional game.

It was, by any stretch, a seminal moment in Irish sport, with clubs and individuals from around the country joining the Thursday afternoon march.

Back at base, players were becoming more agitated. The matter was raised at team meetings and it was decided to leave it to players to attend the march if they wished but they were not under obligation and we would not go there as a squad.

"I think nearly all of the players went on the march," said Peter Bracken. "We all had our own choice. We were not expected to be there but most lads went. Most of us were young and the whole thing didn't affect me as much as maybe the more senior players, the likes of Eric Elwood and Dan McFarland who were married and had children. It was their career and it was a worrying for them. A lot of us felt we would get a position somewhere else but we didn't want to see Connacht being got rid of and all the good work go down the drain. But this wasn't the sort of thing you could prepare for."

Jerry Flannery had broken through into the team that season and both he and the team were going places until the saga broke.

"Eric set the standard for everything, he was constantly working. We were all the same age and most of us were single so all we wanted to do was train and win games; it was a good environment.

"I remember when we went to Donnybrook and Leinster had a rock-star team. Brian O'Driscoll was out but they had everyone else, Gordon D'Arcy had a blue mohawk, he stuck his tongue out at the cameras on the way out. That was my first competitive start. I remember getting into the zone so much, we were smoking them in the lineout and we won the match with a late drop goal from Mark McHugh. We won a lot of tight matches that season and we were moving.

Eric Elwood at the protest march to the IRFU headquarters

Former Minister Mary O'Rourke TD on the march

"I didn't believe that they would get rid of Connacht. I remember going up on that march and some of the players were saying: 'try not to get our pictures taken', that the lads in the union would get pissed off at you for marching against them. Somebody was taking my picture and I was thinking I can't go after him and take the camera off him, but I looked pissed off in the picture. I was a man on a mission."

Michael Swift already had experience of a club getting into serious difficulty in the professional era when Richmond went into administration in England and while his parents were Irish, the London-born forward wasn't too familiar with the set-up in Ireland.

"I didn't know the political system with how Connacht was treated. I had heard of the other provinces more. They had been more successful at that time. I didn't realise how bad it was until that season and when we started hearing rumours. It was the early days of the internet and it took a while for it to gather pace. You can imagine what it would be like now in the media, but it was different then. It was a slow build up. The numbers didn't crunch but it was a harrowing time for a lot of the players.

"I often hear about the strength and unity of Connacht and the up-against-it mentality. But the most emotional speech back then actually came from Dan McFarland. Here he was, like me, an English guy, but he spoke from the heart. Dan mentioned the unity that we had as a group of people, that he made the sacrifice to come over with his family to live and work in Galway. How the powers that be were trying to take that away from him and everyone else.

"I think that is what started our bond with the Connacht and Galway community that we see today. There was a connection there, they had taken us in, us foreigners, guys with English accents.

"And then everyone else jumped on it and then on the day of the march it was something special. The Galway folk living in Dublin, they all turned up. A lot more people turned up than we thought was possible. Looking back, it came very close to being wrapped up. Even now I don't even know how close it came. But it was clear it was on the table," said Swift.

Billy Glynn was convinced it was still on the table after the march. He threatened to go down a legal route and made it clear he would fund it if necessary. The march had grabbed a lot of headlines but he saw nothing to suggest that the threat was easing.

An added factor was that Don Crowley of Galwegians was then president of the IRFU and many in Connacht felt the threat was being pushed at this time to leave him in an invidious position. Weight would be added to the vote to get rid of Connacht simply by virtue of the fact that a man from the province was in the top position.

But the union's trump card ended up being Connacht's ace in the pack.

"They would have lived with the march, treated it as a sort of seven-day wonder," added Glynn. "But I strongly suspect that they were concerned that the president would have to resign.

"I think that was the key, but it was never spoken of. But suddenly the whole thing collapsed. They had overcome the storm of the march, that was gone, that was history.

"What was the next step? Something happened and it is my belief that the issue of resignation of the president of the IRFU was very much to the forefront.

"And that was something they could never live with. That was going to take it outside of Ireland, it was going to take the talking outside of Ireland and don't forget the Six Nations was about to start.

"It was very unfair to Don. They took advantage at the time. They thought that would be something that would

be to their advantage but in fact it turned out to be a disadvantage because I suspect the question of the resignation of the president was very much to the forefront.

"There was never any explanation for them changing their mind. Nothing had changed, their allegedly good reasons for getting rid of Connacht were still all there and suddenly they changed their mind.

"When the Connacht question came up at the committee meeting there would be silence around the table, but I could understand it. They were all hemorrhaging money and they saw this as more money in the kitty. That's the long and the short of it and I could understand their position.

"And, you see, we weren't making any contribution and it took us a long time before we did.

"Nobody around the table was saying that it was a great idea to get rid of Connacht or anything like that. They just sat back, the top table was leading it. There was no question of anyone standing up and saying this was good idea or a bad idea. It was a case of head down, keep looking at the shoelaces, this will all happen and we will all have more money.

"But the fear of the president resigning pulled them back. It was a chance they couldn't take," added Glynn.

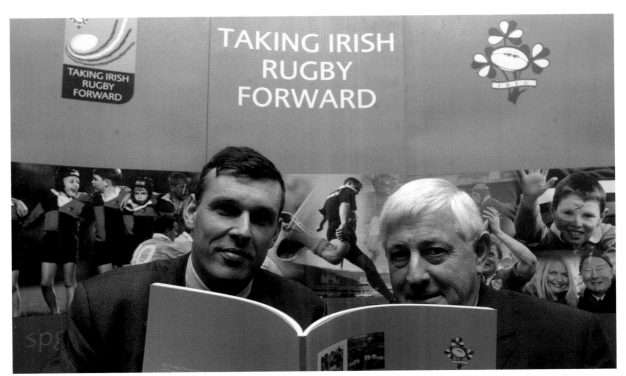

IRFU chief executive Philip Browne and John Hussey, chairman of the IRFU's Strategic Planning Group at the launch of the plan in July 2003

CHAPTER FIVE
Presidential Coup

Don Crowley is one of life's gentlemen, and a man who had worked as an engineer in enough hotspots around the globe to be able to sense danger from afar. However the last place he expected to be hit by a sniper was back in Ireland, after he became the president of the IRFU.

He was born and bred in Galway city centre and after receiving his education through a well-established route of the 'Mon', the 'Bish' and UCG, he set off on an adventurous working life which took him initially to the UK and then on to Libya, Malta, Gibraltar, Sierra Leone and Cameroon.

He picked up a love of rugby while growing up in Galway and though the foreign working fields presented him with little opportunity to further his playing career or to fulfill his desire to go down the coaching route, he immersed himself in Galwegians when he returned in the early 1970s, after more than a decade and a half of building roads, tunnels, bridges, airports and other projects in far-flung places.

His wife Vicki, a renowned artist, is from Malta and he met her in Benghazi when he was working in Libya. Don and Vicki had moved on by the time her family was forced to flee Libya, leaving their businesses behind, after Gaddafi came to power.

The couple and their ever-increasing family moved to Gibraltar, where he oversaw a project building a water reservoir for the British military inside the Rock.

"It was an interesting job. The Rock of Gibraltar is not solid at all. You know how people say: 'As solid as the Rock of Gibraltar'; well it's a warren of tunnels and roadways. It's honeycombed. There are more paved roads inside the Rock of Gibraltar than there are outside. They are mainly military roads so nobody is allowed in, you need a pass, and NATO had a big place in there the time I was there."

He returned to Ireland and set up his own firm, quickly immersing himself in Galwegians where he hoped to become a coach, but he was steered towards administration and in time worked his way through the committee rooms: from the club to Connacht and on to the IRFU, where he was elected president of the union for the 2002-03 season.

It should have been the pinnacle of his sporting career, a year to enjoy holding the top office in Irish rugby, and like all before him, a fitting reward for his life's work.

The union has often had to deal with awkward situations, such as the Troubles in the north or apartheid in South Africa, and while the growing cost of the professional game was a cause for concern, the union looked as solid as most supposed the Rock of Gibraltar to be as they headed into the 2002-03 season.

That, unfortunately, was not long changing. Discussions around meeting the cost of professionalism were focusing more on where costs could be reduced rather than where revenue streams could be developed, and heads were turning towards Connacht.

Nothing, of course, was straight out in the open. Something would be mentioned in one area, and Crowley noticed that by the time he heard it again, it had grown wings.

Things started to come to a head in November when the 22 committee members and the officers of the union met for a think-tank discussion on how to deal with their growing financial difficulties.

"In November 2002 there was a meeting held under the West Stand in Lansdowne Road. The format of the meeting was that there were 25-26 of us maybe, including officers and including those guys who were working for the union.

"We were broken up into six tables of around four each and I had a floating job, I was allowed to go round to all six tables. Except one of the tables was over in 62 Lansdowne Road and I didn't go there. I would just go and listen and put my piece to each of the tables. The reason I didn't go over to 62 Lansdowne Road was because I knew the person chairing that table was Billy Glynn. And Syd Miller was there and he was backing us. So I had no real reason to go there because I knew the lads were there. So I was working the other tables."

"They were discussing the broader vision but the kernel was Connacht. The idea was to get a consensus approach and then go to the union committee and have it sold there. That was the idea.

"I think they had a notion that by the 31st of December that we would be a non-entity.

"It was purely members of the IRFU committee and the officers of the union committee. There were no

IRFU president
Don Crowley
in 2003

branch members there unless they were there already as members of the committee."

"Nobody had the gumption to come to me face-to-face to tell me what they were really thinking. But it was all about Connacht," said Crowley.

It began to dominate everything else and what should have been the pinnacle of Crowley's sporting life became the complete opposite.

"It was the worst period of my life. There were five weeks there that was the worst period of my life, right up to Christmas Day, you know. I was holding a meeting with the officers every week to stop the rumbling and to hold it. It was on the agenda but it was never voted on. I kicked it to touch.

"I knew that if it had gone to a vote of the IRFU, we would have been defeated. So I did my level best and succeeded in not allowing that vote to take place.

"It detracted a lot from the presidency. It made me very wary of people that I shouldn't have been wary of. You're almost afraid to rock the boat."

Two presidents, both from Connacht as it happened, had died in office. Johnny Glynn from Galwegians died in January 1959 and Jim Keane from Athlone passed away shortly after taking office in 1975.

But there had never been an incident of an IRFU president resigning in office and as the saga dragged on it became apparent this might happen.

And, ultimately, the fear that the IRFU president would resign was what saved Connacht in the end.

Don Crowley is adamant about one point – he never threatened to resign.

But he is equally clear that he would have walked away from the presidency the moment Connacht were disbanded.

"I didn't threaten to resign. I would never have threatened that. I'd just have walked.

"You see, the reason they were going for me the time I was there was that if they proved that they got their way to Connacht, all they had to do was point up and say: 'Your man is from Connacht. He's the president. What do you expect?' So that was the last card."

But the downgrading of Connacht had been going on for years and with the finances in a mess, more stringent action was being encouraged.

"When the European Cup came in, there was a two tier competition. The French and the English did their best to commandeer it all. The Italians and ourselves and the Welsh and Scotland were hanging on by a thread so a second tier was created and we, Connacht, were one of the second tier."

President Mary McAleese with IRFU president Don Crowley in 2002

"We were downgraded without anyone ever announcing it. Nobody ever announced it because these meetings were taking place for two-and-a-half years.

"The IRFU finances had taken a big toll because we were paying players for the first time and there was not much money coming in that wasn't there before. They felt that we were the least of the provinces in terms of resources, in terms of players coming through, in terms of people playing for Ireland or whatever else.

"But they weren't saying this up front, they weren't spelling it out. But you knew it from conversations."

Christmas came and went but the Connacht situation didn't go away. If anything, there seemed to be more determination to bring matters to a head but Crowley refused to budge.

"I told them, 'I'm not going to propose it. One of you guys is going to have to propose it. And if you propose it, I will object to it and I don't care what happens. I'm not going to stand up in front of the committee of the IRFU and propose that Connacht should be got rid of.' This was not long before the march.

"I didn't go up to the march purposely because I didn't think it would be of any use. Maybe I would put up the backs of some people I was pulling in. I was working very hard on the trustees of the union.

"There was support there and shortly after that one of them, Syd Millar, spoke at an officers meeting and said: 'Look, it's about time all you guys around this table pull back from the brink.' Those were the exact words he used."

And that was it. The Six Nations was just a few weeks away, Irish rugby didn't need its murky business getting an airing on the international scene and within days a statement was being prepared saying that the professional game would continue as before with a review of Connacht a year later.

But Crowley said that was not accurate and the possible review 12 months down the line was not agreed.

"No, that was never the case. They might have said that in the press but that's nonsense.

"It was a nasty time. It just cut the legs from under me in presidency. I would have walked straight out the door if they got rid of Connacht, there and then but I never threatened anybody with that.

"They thought I would never dream of resigning. And then if I didn't, that was fuel for them to say: 'Well, it happened despite a Connacht man as president, what are you talking to us about?'

"It was very lonely for me to be president at those

Colm Rigney in action against Pontypridd during the 2002-03 Challenge Cup

occasions at the top table because I knew in my heart and soul that if it went to a vote, we had only a handful of votes. The rest of them would have looked down at their feet.

"And if it went, it would be gone forever."

The start of the Six Nations ensured that the focus switched from Connacht fairly rapidly after the decision in late January 2003 to leave the status quo the same.

But it had taken a toll. Friendships, built over the decades, were broken, some never to be mended. But life began to move on for all parties.

"Certainly there was a degree of normality for the remainder of the time that I was president, from when it was decided that Connacht were going to be safe.

"But all we were saying all along is that we're all here for the same reason, we're promoting rugby and the game of rugby. You can't take away the showcase, the team in the shop window. We told them we don't have the numbers in Connacht but there are numbers there and we can nurture the numbers."

One number that sums it all up stands out for him.

All the rancour and all the hard work was made worthwhile when Connacht won the Pro12 title, but for Don Crowley, the really emotional moment came in March when Ireland defeated Italy in the Six Nations and on the field at the end were five Connacht players.

It was the first time ever that five Connacht men played for Ireland at the same time – Robbie Henshaw, Kieran Marmion, Finlay Bealham, Nathan White and Ultan Dillane.

When he was taking about Connacht having numbers when they were trying to stave off extinction, never in his wildest dreams could Crowley see the day when one-third of an Irish winning team would be made up of men from the west. It made everything worthwhile.

"When I saw the five guys out there and they got that photograph taken, I wept like a baby. I was at the match and to see those five guys – Jeepers tonight! And then Connacht to win the Pro12...but when I saw those five guys...I just could never see that day coming.

"They had damaged me so badly about Connacht that I was even doubting myself. But I never doubted Connacht, I was doubting that the building of the bricks would take longer. We had to keep it alive. Now Connacht is vindicated."

It wouldn't have happened had Crowley not stood his ground, holding more steady than the Rock of Gibraltar he had been tunneling through all those years before.

FAMOUS FIVE...Connacht players Kieran Marmion, Nathan White, Finlay Bealham, Ultan Dillane and Robbie Henshaw after guiding Ireland to victory against Italy in the Six Nations in March 2016

Connacht centre Darren Yapp offloads as Munster's Mike Mullins moves in to challenge in the 2002 Celtic League quarter-final in Cork

Exiles' representatives and former Connacht players Phelim McLoughlin (left) and John O'Driscoll (right) with Don Crowley at the IRFU AGM in 2006

CHAPTER SIX
October 2015

The Rugby World Cup continued to disrupt the fixture schedule during the month of October but Connacht still played four games that month.

It turned out to be a bountiful period with four straight wins, three of them at home, as they moved up to second in the table by the time the All Blacks beat Australia to win the World Cup on 31 October.

The month kicked off with a tricky home tie against Cardiff Blues, who had turned into a bogey team since Connacht beat them in their first two meetings when the league began a decade and a half earlier.

Connacht scored a memorable 6-3 win when the sides met on the opening weekend of the league back in 2001 at the Arms Park. The following season, Connacht won 23-22 at the Sportsground, but had only managed three wins in 24 clashes going into this one.

It's a fixture where Connacht never enjoyed much luck, as evidenced by their clash in March earlier in 2015 when Cardiff snatched a controversial late winner in the Arms Park, having earlier in the season come back from the dead to grab a 24-24 draw in the Sportsground.

It turned out to be another high scoring encounter with Connacht holding an edge throughout the 80 minutes, even if the Blues never gave up and secured a late bonus point.

Kieran Marmion got the first of five Connacht tries, with Nepia Fox-Matamua scoring for the third game in a row. Danie Poolman wasn't outdone and he, too, touched down for the third game in succession for Connacht to lead 19-17 at the break at the Sportsground.

Connacht had to come from behind to seal the win but Tiernan O'Halloran and Aly Muldowney got over the line to confirm a 36-31 success.

It was a superb start to his Connacht career for Fox-

STRETCH 1...Kieran Marmion's shirt is tested against Cardiff Blues

STRETCH 2...Quinn Roux hauls Tom McCartney off the ground at the Sportsground

Matamua but the Auckland native played down his try-per-game exploits.

"I just aim to play consistently good rugby and keep pushing to make the starting side.

"There is plenty of rugby to play. As a team, we want to qualify for the Champions Cup and finish as high as we can in the Pro12, and they are the main objectives for the season," he said.

The busy schedule meant that while Connacht might like to take each game as it happened, they needed to look at blocks of games, both in terms of targets and using their playing resources.

And Lam was keen to throw down the gauntlet to his men after their encouraging start.

The Zebre game was the start of a 16-match run in successive weeks and, having won all six previous league meetings against the Parma side, another victory would be the perfect start to a run of ten games in the Pro12 and six in Europe to the end of January.

But with games also due for the Eagles in the B&I Cup and inter-pros, Lam and the other coaches needed to

It was a superb start to his Connacht career for Fox-Matamua but the Auckland native played down his try-per-game exploits.

manage their resources over the next four months.

"We spoke about it at our team meeting. These are exciting times now, at the end of the day we are all in the game to play the game. The challenge is to make every day, every training session, every meeting, everything that we do – make it a winner.

"There is a big management process around it. You are trying out a plan, and also where guys can get opportunities in games. We are going to see more of each other than we will our families so we have got to manage that time.

"There are the four games before Europe. We have now got three home games and one away game. So we look at those first and then we go into two games in Europe.

"It is just all about Zebre, and getting the win here at home against them first," said Lam.

Connacht, for the third game in a row, surpassed the 30-point mark to oust the Italians 34-15, with a superb opening half performance paving the way for the victory.

Matt Healy, Kieran Marmion and Eoin McKeon all crossed for tries, with the boot of Craig Ronaldson opening up a 29-10 interval lead, before Denis Buckley

BLOODIED BUT UNBOWED...Tom McCartney takes aim at a lineout

CHAPTER SEVEN
The Aftermath

Michael Swift remembers the meeting vividly. It took place in the Backstage Bar in the Radisson Hotel one afternoon. We had held many team meetings, jersey presentations and other events in that room during the season but this, by far, was the most emotional and highly charged.

The hullabaloo over the march and Connacht's future had died down a few weeks earlier. Our playing season was over, we were out of Europe and while players were lining out for their clubs at the weekend, they trained with Connacht during the week, with plans being made for next season.

The general gist of what emanated from the IRFU after the threat of disbandment was lifted, was 'carry on as usual', although it was clear that one-year contracts were all that were available. You were almost afraid to mention budgets, in case they were reduced.

Players didn't know what to do. Leaving aside the off-field situation, it had been a good season and their potential didn't go unnoticed by other clubs. And you couldn't blame them for exploring other options, not least when there might be a two or three-year deal on the cards with better money. Why would anyone stick around at a club which might again have its very existence called into question next season?

Contract talks with players dragged on. The format was that Steph Nel would decide who he wanted retained and the chief executive, Gerry Kelly, and I would sit down and try to negotiate a deal. It wasn't easy for any of the parties.

We needed to nail down a squad and move on, but you couldn't blame a player for hedging his bets and waiting to see if something better would come along. Some of them had offers from other clubs and were also talking to others.

The whole area of player agents had not been formalised. They were not registered and it was not unusual to get a call from two people separately, both claiming to be a particular player's agent. It was a mess, the whole lot of it.

The Six Nations was dominating the media coverage and the Connacht story had disappeared.

A number of players had told us that they were moving on. It was the main topic in the dressing room. Some lads were embellishing the offers, if indeed any, they might be getting elsewhere and even those who intended staying with Connacht were reluctant to sign until they saw who else was making the commitment. The whole thing just dragged on and on.

We needed to make firm plans for the following season, so we decided to confront it at the next team meeting. Once the usual issues of the day were discussed, Steph then asked those players who were not staying with us for next season to stand up and leave as we needed to talk about preparing for the following campaign.

"I remember when Steph goes: 'guys who are leaving, now can you please leave the room, we need to talk about next season'. There was absolute silence because nobody expected it," said Swift.

"I remember seeing Colm (Rigney) leaving, Gavin (Duffy) as well. I was like: 'wow, okay'. I was aware at that stage who was leaving but it's like all things, when you see things happening in front of you and guys getting up, and it was a lot of our better players, it was startling.

"We used to have meetings and pre-match food in that bar in the Radisson. And this was like turning the page into the next phase of Connacht rugby. They were worrying times.

"I had a couple of offers, nothing out of this world. Looking back, if I am brutally honest, if I had a really good offer from another team, would I have gone? Maybe. But there was a lot of uncertainty and you can't blame some of these guys for going. What was to say that it wouldn't happen again, if you have got your employers basically saying that they are not sure if they want to employ you?" said Swift.

Asking the players to leave the meeting was a horrible, but necessary, step to take as we simply had to

> *'I remember when Steph goes: 'guys who are leaving, now can you please leave the room, we need to talk about next season'. There was absolute silence because nobody expected it.'*

Michael Swift in action in 2002

move on. Steph and I were standing at the top of the room facing the players and could see who was getting up to leave, but we weren't sure who was going to get up and go.

We knew some who were leaving but were glancing in the direction of some others, silently saying: 'don't f**king stand up!' while the players, sitting in rows, had to look around to find out who was going and who was staying.

A lot of key players left: No. 8 Colm Rigney went to Leeds Tykes; Jerry Flannery and Eoin Reddan were snapped up by their native Munster; Gavin Duffy went to Harlequins; and Johnny O'Connor went to Wasps. One-third of the starting team gone in one swoop, four of whom went on to become full Irish senior internationals. There were others who later departed as well, who hadn't deals signed off at that point, but that was a defining day.

Steph, although he knew about most of the departures, was devastated. Three years work down the drain, and for what? I joined him on one of the balconies at the hotel, where he had his pipe going like a steam train. He didn't fault the players, not in the least, but he knew it could, and should, have been so different. He didn't say anything but by the time we left the balcony I

just knew he would not be at the Sportsground the next season, even if he had a year of his contract to go.

It was a horrible day, one that made you question your own involvement, as the wedges started to appear in a group which had been rock solid. I knew how the players felt.

Jerry Flannery's ambition was to get back home to Limerick and play for Munster and Ireland, but he is adamant that had circumstances been different, the Connacht team of that time would have become the first to win silverware for the province.

"There's no doubt if we stayed together as a group, that team could have gone on and won things. I have no doubt about it. If you look at the Munster teams that won stuff, the reason they did was because they kept the group together. For years that team stuck together: Horan, Hayes, O'Callaghan, O'Connell, Leamy, Foley, Quinlan, Williams, Wallace, Stringer, O'Gara, and so on. If a team stays together for a long time, and you get the right guys in there to drive the culture of the club, you are going to be successful. When I look at the Connacht team that I played on, if that team stuck together could it have been successful? Yeah, 100 per cent, I have no doubt.

"It was incredible, I remember we trained with a real

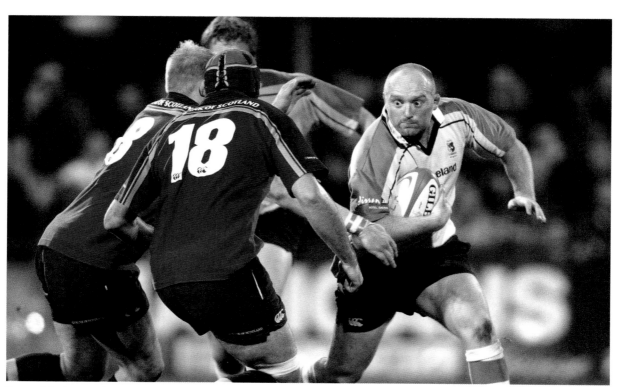

Bernard Jackman takes on Leinster's Des Dillon (left) and Aidan Kearney in 2003

PENSIVE...Connacht coach Steph Nel deep in thought

chip on our shoulders. There were so many of us of the same age, most of us were between 20 and 23. We trained insanely hard. Des Ryan was the trainer, and we were so fit. When I went down to Munster the following year with Eoin Reddan and Martin McPhail, we were blitzing people when it came to conditioning.

"We used to go out to the hills in Oranmore for pre-season with Connacht. I still have the photos. I remember doing those sessions and Johnny O'Connor used to go ballistic, trying to be the best. Myself and Redser (Eoin Reddan) said we would try stick with Johnny and we wouldn't be far off. There would be ten different competitions in the black session, gruelling stuff, and Johnny would win nine of them. Someone would beat him on the tenth and he would go mad! It was brilliant, guys were driving each other on. We would have won something, I have absolutely no doubt about it, had we stuck together.

"I wasn't going around saying I had these offers but I knew the foreign players and even some of the Irish guys were saying they had these offers and were weighing them up. Everyone wants to sound good in front of their peers. I remember the nagging feeling all of the time I played with Connacht was that I had to leave here to be successful. When the IRFU said they were

going to cut the funding and get rid of Connacht, that puts a rocket under your ass to say you have to move out of here. But it was a bit depressing the way it happened," said Flannery.

Everyday life went on for players, management, officials and supporters amidst all the chaos. In my own case, my father was in hospital at the time and I used to visit him each morning on the way into work and again in the evening, heading home. He was struggling to recover from routine surgery, but for a man who had been diagnosed with cancer and given six to twelve months to live 17 years earlier, there wasn't'thuge concern on that evening of 24 April 2003.

On my way out of the Sportsground I decided to head out to Oranmore where Steph Nel lived. I had, mistakenly, felt that he wasn't doing enough to persuade players to stay and wanted to have it out with him. Steph had given his heart and soul to Connacht for three years and had felt very let down, especially as he had built such a promising squad. He had enough of Ireland by then.

We had a bit of a row but, as always with Steph, everything was sorted out, he smoked his pipe and offered me a glass of red and after a few hours we parted on good terms.

Jerry Flannery prepares for a lineout against Leinster in 2002

It was late when I got to the hospital but not long after arriving it was apparent my dad was going downhill. Within an hour he died. Just like that, an hour and a bit short of his 75th birthday.

Steph was distraught when he rang me the following morning but, as I pointed out to him, if it wasn't for the IRFU threat to disband Connacht and all that ensued I would probably have gone home much earlier and not been with my dad when he died.

Steph and all the players turned up at the funeral a couple of days later in their number ones and I have often thought my dad would have got a laugh out of that. He was a GAA man from Castlegar, the most prolific winners of the Galway hurling championship, and he had little interest in 'the rugby', although he was an admirer of Willie John McBride. He was a great man for going to funerals but if he had ever given thought to what sort of send-off he might receive himself, the attendance of a professional rugby squad was hardly one he envisaged.

Steph stepped down as Connacht coach a few days after that, returning to South Africa, although he returned to the northern hemisphere the following December for a stint with Rotherham Titans.

The following week Gerry Kelly and I headed to Dublin to meet Eddie Wigglesworth, the IRFU director of rugby.

The threat of disbandment may have been lifted, for now at least, but Connacht were now without a coach and a host of frontline players. The furore had died down, the banners had been put away and people went about their usual business. Some protesters, having been vocal in how important it was to save Connacht, never bothered going to a match after that.

It was often thrown back at Connacht that if everyone who marched to the IRFU headquarters turned up at matches on a regular basis, then maybe the province wouldn't have been in such difficulty in the first place. It was hard to argue with that.

If Eddie Wigglesworth felt that way, then he kept his thoughts to himself. Gerry had warned me on the way up to Dublin in the car that I might be in for a bit of a bollicking. We knew Wigglesworth was being blamed for the newspaper leak which brought the threat of the disbandment into the public domain in the first place but he, too, would have known my fingerprints were across a lot of the stuff which Connacht threw back at them in the media.

It didn't really matter to me as I did not intend for it to be a permanent career move, but if Wigglesworth had any ill-feeling it was not apparent. In fact, he could

Fitness coach Des Ryan

Peter Bracken gets stuck into Harlequins in 2004

hardly have been more helpful and courteous at that hotel meeting. I thought it was very admirable and it set the tone needed to get the show back on the road.

Wigglesworth had compiled a list of names of players whom he felt might be ready for a move to Galway. We had gone with a wish list as well and by the time we broke up there was the makings of a decent squad, if even half of them were signed up for the 2003-04 season.

And it wasn't just players who had occupied Wigglesworth's mind; he also suggested a coach and that was when Michael Bradley – who still remains Connacht's longest serving coach in the professional era – first entered the equation.

Bradley, a former Irish scrum-half with 40 caps, half of them as captain, had guided his home club Cork Constitution to All-Ireland League glory before being appointed the Ireland U-21 coach. He was in Scotland watching Ireland take part in the Four Nations Youth (U-18) tournament when he got the call to come home as the union might have other plans for him if Connacht were agreeable.

Gavin Duffy in action against Pontypridd in 2003

"I was a young coach so I was quite comfortable being told where to go, in that sense. It was a secondment as well. It wasn't like: 'You're going to be head coach of Connacht for seven years.' It was a one-year secondment.

"I was employed by the union, so it wasn't a case of giving up a job. I presumed I would have gone back into the 21s because they would have been seen as critical to the cause of the national side.

"It was difficult in Connacht. There were a lot of unselfish decisions made by a lot of players around that time because they would have been getting offers from elsewhere.

"I would have been very familiar with the Munster set-up in particular and the set-up with Ireland and how players were dealt with. There was a fair gap between the opportunities that the Connacht players had compared to the other provinces.

"That really kicked in about half way through the first year when it was clear it was not like with like. For the next period of the time everything we tried to do was to have Connacht considered as one of four teams, as opposed to three and one. That was what we always tried to work on.

"Look at the budgets. It wasn't possible to hold on to the players. Retention was hard. If a player plays well and he has two good seasons, you have the other three provinces actively coming in. The agents had knowledge of all budgets and knew what they could get for their man.

"Once we started to get a bit of momentum, from my point of view, we couldn't compete with the financial side of it. But what Connacht could compete on was the sense of connection with the province and the club itself, the club being the people who were in it at the time and around it. There is substance and there is quality in that and if you can get that into a team, even though it's intangible, it's not unlike Leicester with the Premier League. People are wondering: 'How did they do that? They don't have the money to buy the players.' They're not buying players, they're producing a team. Rugby, first and foremost, is a team game. Connacht, certainly back then, didn't have world-class facilities or the budget, but they had a sense of identity. And that was key," said Bradley.

Bernard Jackman returned to Connacht after his stint with Sale Sharks, working his way back into the professional game via Clontarf, and he found that both Connacht and the Celtic League were changed environments when he returned in the summer of 2003.

"Things were a lot better, Connacht had changed a lot.

It was a good opportunity for me to play. We were better in the Challenge Cup, but we struggled with consistency.

"When I went to Sale Sharks the facilities over there were top of the range. They were playing in a league that had already got a track record. If you look back to the Celtic League then, you played Celtic Warriors, they went out of business. There was no history there of rivalry. There was inter-provincial rivalry but again, it was all new. Go to play the Dragons, Connacht didn't have anything against the Dragons. Whereas Sale against Leicester, Sale against Harlequins, you go back 70 years and that was in place so the Premiership had that. They had the TV deal. They had good crowds and they were a long way ahead of us in terms of professionalism.

"Now, the Irish eventually caught up. Munster didn't have the most professional set-up, but they found a way of competing. Connacht hadn't yet found their niche.

"The schedule was much better when I came back. The season was more fluid. There were less games for your club and that was important. You only played the odd game for your club if you were coming back from injury. We trained hard, we did our pre-season on that hill in Oranmore or in UCG, down by the river. Then we would go all around the province. Connacht is a beautiful region and it was great to get out and train in Sligo or Mayo or wherever.

"But we just struggled to be consistent. I think Connacht always worked harder. There was a better work ethic in Connacht and that's going back to when Des Ryan was the fitness coach there. We used to test more than the other provinces, there was much more focus on it. In the old days, the provinces used to go up to Santry to be tested and our scores would wipe the boards with Leinster, Munster and Ulster but they'd be the guys that got picked to play for Ireland.

"So we were fitter, stronger in most cases because we actually probably worked harder, but we struggled to transfer that to the pitch.

"Connacht had that culture of work ethic and that's still there. That's the ace in the pack that they had and they still have," said Jackman.

The return of the likes of Jackman and several other good signings meant that Connacht were in decent fettle heading into the 2003-04 but while it turned out to be a reasonable season for the province, the highlight being a tremendous two-leg Challenge Cup semi-final battle with Harlequins which was narrowly lost, the prospect of silverware, which had arisen prior to the threat of disbandment, was further off now than ever.

Eric Elwood and Michael Bradley against Ospreys in 2005

CHAPTER EIGHT
November 2015

In any other campaign, a first win over Munster in the professional era at Thomond Park would rank as a seasonal highlight but, in a season packed with so many notable events, it wasn't even the standout moment of the month.

That belonged to the trip to Siberia, a first ever for a professional club side. The trip to Krasnoyarsk for a European Challenge Cup clash with Enisei-STM will never be forgotten by those who made the arduous journey through seven times zones and temperatures of minus 25 degrees Celsius.

Ireland travelled there for a World Cup qualifier in 2002 but that was played in September and the difference in temperature in the space of a few months is unreal.

The Russian rugby season is from April to September and they don't play during the winter months because the weather is so inhospitable in Siberia, but they had to conform with the EPCR schedule.

It looked like Connacht drew the short straw when they were drawn into a pool featuring Newcastle Falcons and Brive, before any thought was given to the question of traveling to Krasnoyarsk, the homeland of Russian rugby. Yet the odyssey turned out to be a blessing in disguise and contributed hugely in developing the team spirit which served Connacht so well as the season progressed.

The Russian champions, featuring in European competition for the first time, wanted their three pool games in their home city Krasnoyarsk, which is a five-hour flight east of Moscow.

But the EPCR wanted them played at the more accessible Winter Olympic city Sochi, close to the Georgian border, and that's where Newcastle and Brive played them. It was agreed that Enisei-STM would play one home match and Connacht were drawn to make that trip.

Enisei-STM may have been new to the tournament but they were familiar with Connacht as they had travelled to Galway several times to play the Connacht Eagles.

But nothing could have prepared the travelling party for the trip to Krasnoyarsk, a city of about one million people on the Yenisei River and just south of the Gulag Peninsula.

A small group consisting of the squad, three members of the media – Linley MacKenzie from the Galway Advertiser and James Crombie from Inpho Photography were on board along with myself – and an EPCR representative, constituted the travelling party which left Shannon for Moscow on a charter flight on a wet Tuesday evening in November.

The match was on Saturday afternoon and, given the time zones, we were due back in Shannon on the charter flight on Saturday night. Instead the last of us got home in dribs and drabs the following Tuesday night, having come via several cities after our aircraft broke down on the ground in the extreme temperatures.

A refueling stop in Moscow on the way out was followed by another five-hour flight over endless snow-covered mountains until we arrived in Krasnoyarsk some time on Wednesday.

It was sunny on arrival but the extreme weather became obvious soon after we boarded the team bus for the lengthy trip to the city. The bus was warm when we got on and we were all looking forward to seeing the sights on the way to the hotel.

But within minutes condensation hit the windows and froze solid; it was as if somebody had painted the windows white and completely blocked out the view. You needed a coin or something to scrape it away to get a view but within minutes it would again be frozen. And the heater was on in the bus!

We had all come prepared for the cold and, in fairness, daytime temperatures in the sun were akin to a skiing trip, but when you went in the shade or came out at night it was just astounding; each breath seemed to

> *Within minutes condensation hit the windows and froze solid; it was as if somebody had painted the windows white and completely blocked out the view. You needed a coin or something to scrape it away to get a view but within minutes it would again be frozen.*

A bloodied Jason Harris-Wright after a clash with Brive in the Challenge Cup

to be drawn up.

The key was to get to Moscow. The travelling party was split up and tentative plans were made for the various groups to go home via a variety of cities. Some made it home by Monday night, the last of us got there by Tuesday evening after a night in Moscow.

The players dealt admirably with the saga, reviewing the Enisei-STM game and plotting for Brive, although John Muldoon did admit that the BO level had reached epic proportions as players ran out of clean clothes!

"It's like a game at the moment, things change during the game, and you just have to adapt," said Lam, while we hung around Sheremetyevo Airport in Moscow, trying to get a flight to some place closer to home.

"It's just been a real challenge, I said it was going to be a mental test and it has been that.

"I am pretty proud of the management and players and everybody is just getting on with it. It's been one challenge after another. We didn't sleep for 30 hours. One day we will look back at it and say it made us tougher."

It was a measure of just how far the trip to Siberia was that when Connacht finally got on their delayed flight to Moscow out of Krasnoyarsk on the Monday, the Enisei-STM team they had defeated were also on board,

starting their journey to play Newcastle Falcons the following Sunday.

Connacht's casualty problems continued to mount with Tom McCartney, John Cooney and Nathan White all picking up injuries in the win over Treviso, but those knocks presented opportunities to others, and hooker Shane Delahunt, another product of the Connacht academy, seized his opportunity.

"The season has started really well. I know we are small squad but everyone knows what we are doing. Everyone is cohesive and working together.

"We know there are going to be rotations made and everyone is going to get some game time in this block of matches. It is something to really look forward to," said the Offaly native.

Rory Parata scored for the second week in a row as Connacht saw off Brive at the Sportsground, with Ben Marshall and Kieran Marmion also touching down in a 21-17 success that made it eight wins from nine matches in all competitions.

But the joy was dampened when it emerged that Fox-Matamua was ruled out for the season with a cruciate injury, while Marshall and Eoin McKeon suffered concussions and Andrew Browne injured a hand.

Even with the mounting injuries, competition was keen

for places and Bundee Aki, now in his second season after joining from the Chiefs, said this created the perfect environment for success.

"I want to play week in, week out, and perform consistently. We are gelling really well at the moment, and just starting to get into our groove. The real challenge is to try and be consistent in how we play.

"There is a lot of competition going on, and it makes it a lot tougher for myself, and for the other lads trying to get into the starting jerseys.

"That is what we need in our team, everyone trying to fight for a jersey which is healthy for us. If you don't play well someone can take your jersey," said Aki.

If the general Irish sporting public were not aware of Aki's ability prior to that, he certainly made them sit up and take notice with an awesome display against Munster which he crowned with the match-clinching try after a superb offload by Robbie Henshaw.

Connacht's only victory ever at Thomond Park was in November 1986 when they won 11-9 on a day when Robbie Henshaw's uncle Davy Henshaw was tighthead prop for the visiting province.

Connacht had only won two of the 26 league meetings between the sides in the professional era but another barrier was knocked down when they finally triumphed in Thomond Park on an 18-12 scoreline.

They led 10-5 thanks to a try from Tiernan O'Halloran and a couple of kicks from Craig Ronaldson, and Aki sealed the win with his superb score in the left corner two minutes from the finish, ending years of frustration for players like prop Ronan Loughney.

"I was talking to John Muldoon afterwards and for me over the last number of years, you associate just a feeling of disappointment with that changing room in Thomond Park. It was great to finally get a win down there.

"Any of the young guys that have had an opportunity: Shane Delahunt, Ultan Dillane and Conan O'Donnell and loads more, they are really putting their hands up any chance they get.

"And that's maybe something that we haven't had in the past, that depth in the squad. The players that are brought on, have had a decent impact and have fitted into the structure well, and have helped us close out games.

"Where in the past we wouldn't have had that help to close it out," said Loughney.

Once again the injuries mounted. Henshaw suffered a metacarpal fracture which would rule him out for six weeks. MacGinty needed surgery on a knee injury which

POIGNANT...Pat Lam and the late Munster coach Anthony Foley at Thomond Park in November 2015

Connacht celebrate after beating Munster in November 2015 at Thomond Park for the first time since 1986

would sideline him for a few weeks, Eoghan Masterson fractured a thumb and Denis Buckley suffered a high-ankle sprain, with both set to miss three weeks of action.

"For us losing any player to injury is tough," said Lam. "We have had a pretty hard run with injuries. But it is one of those things that we have been saying as a squad. What we have been doing is around teamwork and the next guy just steps in.

"We have had eight wins in a row, and the way we look at it, Robbie Hesnhaw's played three of those

games.

"We haven't had the same 15 throughout the whole season. Probably if I marked out, what is on paper, the best 15 we have never been able to put that out. But that is what rugby is. What we do on and off the field is crucial."

Aside from the historic aspect of winning at the Limerick venue, it was also the first time Connacht had won six league games in a row and kept them top of the table heading into December.

Robbie Henshaw and Jack Carty after the win over Munster at Thomond Park

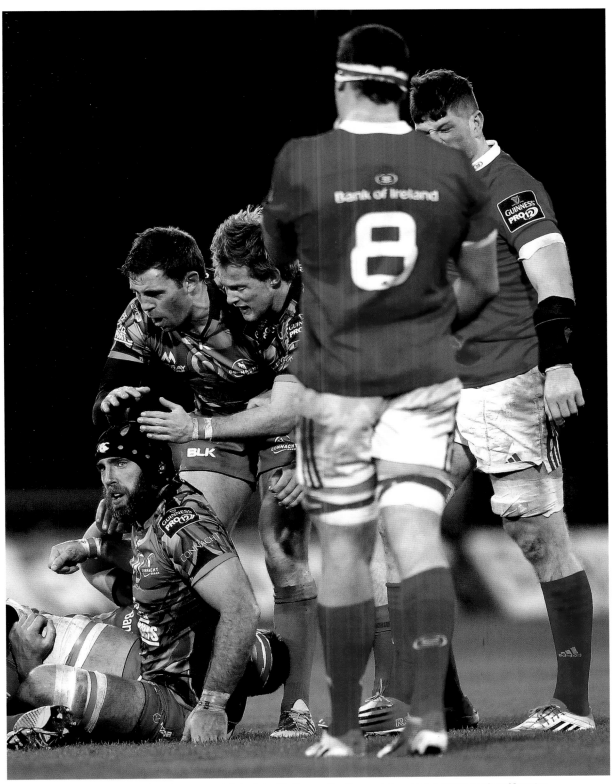

Craig Ronaldson and Kieran Marmion congratulate John Muldoon after the captain won a penalty against Munster

CHAPTER NINE
The Academy

Cillian Gallagher thinks about it for a moment and comes to his conclusion. "It's mad, it really is. Going out in an U-20 Six Nations match and 20 per cent of the starting team coming from Sligo. If you told someone that five years ago they would have said you were crazy."

Gallagher, a 6'5" lock weighing in at over 17 and a half stone, made his debut with the Irish U-20 side as an 18-year-old and will be underage when the World Rugby U-20 Championship is held in Georgia in June 2017.

He was joined in that Six Nations squad by prop Conan O'Donnell, playing his second year in the grade and already capped at senior level by Connacht, and scrum-half Stephen Kerins. A fourth Sligo player, Matthew Cosgrove, came in as a replacement when Gallagher was injured in the 2016 World Rugby U-20 Championship in Manchester.

Sligo has a proud rugby tradition, with Sligo Grammar School and Summerhill College working with Sligo RFC to keep the game alive in the north of the province.

But it was the creation of the Connacht academy in 2004 that opened up a pathway for that talent in Sligo to move to a higher level with the province and with Ireland. Pat Lam immediately recognised the value of the academy when he arrived in Connacht and brought them in to train with the senior squad from the outset of his reign.

It might have made for some crowded sessions but for the emerging talent, this was a huge boost.

Scrum-half Stephen Kerins – a former Sligo minor Gaelic footballer and a cousin of international showjumper Darragh Kerins – said that once a player makes it into the academy, the rest of the journey is laid before you.

"The amount of effort that is put into our academy section is just amazing. You train with the lads, you train in with the senior team, you are always around everyone. When you see those lads breaking through, you are only one or two injuries away from getting into the senior team, you are there or thereabouts. It's just

'I'm thrilled for Ronan. He was very professional in his approach to everything, even back then. He captained the U-21s that year with Connacht. You could see he was already looking ahead.'

an amazing opportunity to be in the Connacht academy.

"Having the opportunity to play with your best friends since you were young, playing all the way through, it just shows all of the work being done in Connacht at the moment. It feeds through into the senior team for Connacht and Sligo, and for everyone. The whole culture in Connacht has changed and it is really reaping the rewards for that," said Kerins.

Gallagher, who has honed his skills playing Gaelic football, soccer and basketball, said that when an academy player makes it to the senior team it is a huge boost for all the other young lads striving for their breakthrough.

"I initially came in for summer camps at U-15 level and stayed involved after that, getting into the sub-academy and working from there.

"In and around the Sportsground every day of the week there is a constant buzz. The fact that we are so close to the senior team, who are doing some great things, is super. They had been floating under the radar but we have seen all of their work when we have been so close to them and it was great to see them get the reward with the Pro12 title. It was a great year to be involved there.

"When you see people like Sean O'Brien, who was training with us in the academy in the summer of 2015, make it – it's a huge boost. He was training with me every day. He played an Eagles game or two with me at the start of the season and you could tell he was way above that".

"He stepped up, and look at the season that he had. As an academy player in Connacht you are definitely not too far away and Pat has said that to all of us. If you are good enough you are old enough and that's the way he sees it. You have to have your head on every day you are in the academy. If injuries come – and Connacht had a big injury list this year – if the call comes we all have to be ready to take that step up."

Seven players stepped up from the academy and played a total of 55 games in the victorious Pro12 campaign and the contributions made by James

THE FUTURE...2015 academy players Cian Romaine, Conor Kyne, Cormac Brennan, Pat O'Toole, Conor Lowndes, Stephen McVeigh and Conan O'Donnell, with academy manager Nigel Carolan

Carolan operated an open door policy with the media. Maybe it would have been different if there were a few of us, but I doubt it. He saw this as a great opportunity for young players to get some media exposure, the same for his coaches. He sent out the message that: 'What you are doing is good, get out there and tell the world'.

Two days before they played England in the final at the AJ Bell Stadium, I went out to the Trafford Metrovick RFC grounds near Sale which was their training base, as I needed to do a couple of short radio interviews.

The players and coaches were about to go into a tactical meeting where they were laying out their plans for the championship final two days later. Carolan suggested I might as well attend the meeting. "You may as well see what we will be trying to do on Saturday. You'll know as the game goes on whether it's working."

His straight-up, 'this-is-what-we-do' approach has been there since he started the academy in 2004 and it was no surprise when it prospered.

"When I got in as the academy manager, it was just an S&C coach and myself. Then we had a number of volunteers and part-timers and development staff that we utilised. Then, as the academy grew, the resources grew with it," said Carolan.

"We constantly looked to expand. We felt A games were vital as they bridged the gap between the club game and the professional game. That was one of the first areas we went after, doing so in 2006. We had to prove then to the IRFU that we could sustain an A team and to do that, we needed to increase the number of academy players we had. It was a double-edged sword."

But it worked. Carolan took charge of the A side, guiding them into the B&I Cup and polishing the young talent more and more for senior rugby. Graduates started to flow from the academy into the senior team and Connacht have not looked back since.

"We had 21 guys contracted to the academy in the 15/16 season, with a staff of 12 or 13, between strength and conditioning, psychology, nutrition, personal development and rugby specialists. Most of them would be working full-time, some of them on contract.

"It widens into sub-academy and the elite structures then that are below that.

"Everything is in the Sportsground. That's the beauty of Connacht. It's small but it's very central. Everybody rubs shoulders together, from the pros to the academy to the sub-academy to the age grade guys, they're all in together."

Carolan has taken pleasure in seeing players come through and make the grade, not just for Connacht but

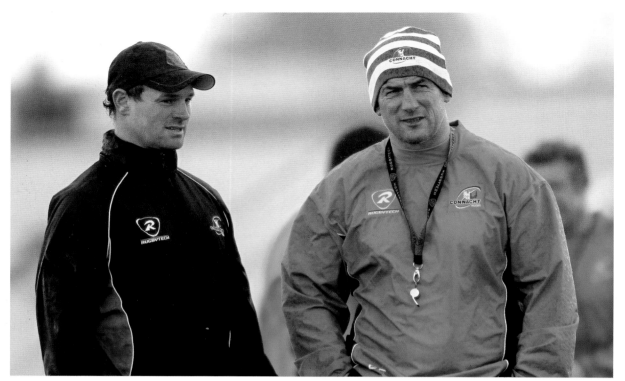

Nigel Carolan and Eric Elwood

for other sides as well.

"The Connacht academy is an Irish rugby programme so it's run in the best interests of Irish rugby. Obviously we hope that we can develop those players up to a level where firstly they make the professional standard and if they can go on and be good enough to play for Ireland, that's good.

"It's grown and in more recent years, the IRFU have seen the need for us to have the adequate resources to be able to look after players, in terms of effective player movement.

"If it was the case that we were to move a player from one of the other provinces to Connacht, or in most cases where a player wasn't going to be picked up by one of the other provinces because of the succession plan or the roadblock positionally, we were in a position then to be able to offer these guys a place. Guys like Mick Kearney would have come to us. Guys like Rory Moloney have come down to Connacht because of the succession plans, the opening we would have and the blockages in the other provinces. Inevitably a lot of them go back, they are not here forever.

"For a player to come to Connacht, he really wanted to believe that there was pathway for him. It wasn't always the case. For most guys at the time, it was traditional

that you stayed with your own province. It wasn't too common to move, particularly so young. It took a really ballsy decision for guys to move, and for the few guys that did, it didn't always pay off. But you'd hope that you give any player that comes into the academy the best opportunity to follow their dreams."

Michael Bradley and Eric Elwood benefited from the talent coming out of the academy but it stepped up a few notches when Pat Lam came on board in 2013. With a staff and playing roster considerably lighter than the teams he was going to be competing with, Lam knew he needed the academy to underpin the whole operation.

"In Pat's first year, due to limited resources, Pat utilised some of the academy staff in sessions and I suppose, he looked to integrate as many of the academy guys as possible," recalled Carolan.

"So in his first year here, most of the time, all of the academy guys were in on top of his guys. I think we had 20 contracted. Sessions were particularly hectic with so many players and academy staff trying to integrate into that. Gradually then we agreed that we should only integrate a certain number of guys at certain stages and we'd prioritise a certain number of positions so that's the way we go about it now.

"For a young guy to crack it, he needs a senior player

to get injured, in some cases two or three injuries, and then to make himself available, and that's where the hard work kicks in. They need to be physically and technically up to a level if and when the chance comes up to bring them, that Pat has the confidence then to give them the chance to play.

"Any player that plays for the pros, it's a temporary basis. It's all part of the development. You've got to keep your feet on the ground. That circumstantial selection doesn't mean that they've actually made it. They have to continue to work on the areas that they need to succeed."

Three out of every four players who get into the Connacht academy will go to play the sport professionally at some level, but getting over the line into the academy can be the most difficult thing for a teenager.

"About 75 per cent of players that come into the academy will engage in a professional context at some stage.

"Every year when we would start at the bottom of our pyramid, we could have 400-500 players at the initial stages, aged around 14 or 15, at the screening stages. When we bring them in it's about resourcing the players with real potential. The IRFU have released their strategic plan, which is in line with Connacht, in resourcing the younger guys as early as possible.

"The objective of the academy, which we set out maybe five or six years ago, not from the outset, was to produce future winning professional rugby players for Connacht that will go on and play for Ireland.

"That winning mentality is about what they do every day. They give themselves the best opportunity every single day to succeed on the field, in terms of the extra skills they need to nurture, the core skills, the professional skills, and off the field looking after their education, their nutrition, their time management. That will enable them to become winners.

"We are fortunate to have excellent support services so every player requiring development in a certain area can access expertise in that area to assist them. For a player to make it now, it's not really by accident – all they're waiting for is a chance. We believe that not everyone is going to make it but every day, if players are looking after their individual plans, then they give themselves the best chance."

He wasn't able to attend the Pro12 final as he was preparing the Irish side for the World Rugby U-20 Championship but he took huge pleasure in the win, not least as Ronan Loughney provided that link back to where the whole academy started.

"I think for guys like him who've been there in the days when things were a lot tougher, it's a culmination of the perseverance, the hard work and the belief to stick to it. I think it's been probably most pleasing for him – he's been a one-club man and he's been very loyal to Connacht, and it's good that players like him get payback for all their hard work.

"I think all the new guys, the young guys that have come through, they've only seen the last couple of years and good structures. They've only seen how hard work can pay off. Hopefully that's breeding good habits into them that they can take forward."

Carolan has played down his own role in the historic success but Gerry Kelly, the chief executive who appointed him, is in no doubt about the contribution he has made to rugby in Connacht.

"We made a lot of good appointments over the years – Brads, Eric and so on – but from a point of view of getting to where we are now Nigel was a huge appointment. He has everything: he is very intelligent, he has a great knowledge of rugby. It was the most significant appointment that we ever made," said Kelly.

Sligo native and academy scrum-half Stephen Kerins

CHAPTER TEN
December 2015

The mood in the Connacht camp was high heading towards the festive season, but everyone knew the tests were about to become more difficult.

Tiernan O'Halloran may have been just 24 years of age but the Clifden native was in his seventh season with Connacht and could gauge what was happening.

"We're not getting carried away. It's just over a third of the way through the Pro12 season. But this season, it feels different around the Sportsground.

"Even just in the changing rooms. There is definitely a good vibe flowing throughout the squad. In training the confidence is there, people are coming out of their shells, and trying things that they might not have tried in the past.

"You can tell people are bouncing at the moment, and that shows in the games. Lads are making massive improvements, and are really standing up and getting noticed. All the way from one to 23, even the bench that come on every week – they are making a massive contribution," he said.

First up in December was a trip to the Arms Park in Cardiff on a night when John Muldoon became the first player in the league to chalk up 200 appearances in the competition.

Current form suggested only one winner, with Connacht going into the Friday evening clash on the back of six league wins in a row and Cardiff coming off seven straight losses after topping the table after round one with a 61-13 thumping of Zebre.

Pat Lam could sense the danger in advance. "Part of the learnings before I came here was that Connacht went 14 games without a win. When that happens to a side you know they are due a win. If we allow them to have that opportunity, they will take it.

"Any team like that are desperate to do anything to win. And so if we open that door and give them that opportunity there is no doubt they will take it."

And that's exactly what Cardiff did on their artificial surface in the shadow of the Millennium Stadium as they carved out a 20-16 victory. Tries from Ian Porter and

Eoin McKeon had Connacht 13-10 in front at the break but Cardiff got on top in the second-half and the only consolation for the visitors came in the closing stages when Jack Carty landed a penalty to secure a bonus point.

But salt was rubbed in the wound with Quinn Roux expected to be out for three months with an ankle injury, while a broken bone in one of his hands finished Darragh Leader's season. An elbow injury threatened to sideline Eoin McKeon for three to four weeks, while both Craig Ronaldson and Kieran Marmion were concussed.

The focus switched back to the European Challenge Cup and experienced prop Ronan Loughney knew they needed to hit back straight away in the back-to-back clashes with Newcastle Falcons.

"There are two massive games coming up. It wasn't a good result in Cardiff – at the end we still had a chance to win it, and it was disappointing that we didn't get over the line.

"It was our processes and stuff that we didn't stick to, and that let us down. It is disappointing that the run has come to an end, but it is up to ourselves how we respond. We have that healthy pressure on ourselves, and it is a massive challenge.

"We love cup rugby, and we have set our sights high in the Challenge Cup. Our next game is a massive game at home. We have that home record to protect," he said.

Connacht, who had played more games than any other side in Europe in the Challenge Cup, won their opening three pool games for only the third time when they defeated the Falcons 25-10 with a fine performance at the Sportsground. It was their 57th win in the competition, having lost 51 and never drawn a tie in the Challenge Cup.

Six penalties from Jack Carty pushed Connacht clear before Danie Poolman got their only try to wrap up the win. The only downside came with yet another concussion injury, Dave McSharry the injured party this time. It would turn out to be his 65th and final game for Connacht in five seasons and he was forced to retire from the game the following August.

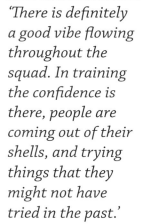

'There is definitely a good vibe flowing throughout the squad. In training the confidence is there, people are coming out of their shells, and trying things that they might not have tried in the past.'

Eoghan Masterson runs out for Connacht at Kingston Park in Newcastle.

CATCH ME...Bundee Aki in full flight against Cardiff

Aly Mudowney, one of the key figures as the 2-4-2 system really took hold, said after the Newcastle win that the strength of the squad was in dealing with injuries as they arose.

"We have had a challenging week on and off the field with the injuries. But we really stuck in there, and the young boys really fronted up.

"All week they have been exceptional and to really stick in the game at the end and deny them anything out of the game was huge for us.

"With the World Cup that has been going on, the congestion of games, it was likely that we would get injuries.

"It was just a chance for us now to prove what our squad can do. Guys are doing great in the academy, those are really helping us by coming through and pushing us on," he said.

The injury crisis, coupled with the restrictions around registering players in European competition, meant that Connacht fielded a squad of just 22 players for the game away to Newcastle the following week.

"These back-to-back games are always interesting," said Lam. "They're like Test matches. We know that we did things well and there are things we didn't do well. There is no surprise element and we go into their back

yard now.

"It's a really good mental test. This is the beauty of the European back-to-back weekends, it's what we can do better this week, knowing full well that they know what's coming."

Victories in England have always been rare for Connacht, with just two wins – against Northampton in 1997 and Worcester Warriors in 2009 – to show from 16 visits to nine clubs in European competitions.

And a depleted Connacht side never looked like improving that record in a Sunday afternoon kick-off where a Danie Poolman try had the sides deadlocked 5-5 at the break, before the Falcons pulled away to win 29-5.

To compound matters, Peter Robb picked up a concussion and hooker Jason Harris-Wright and Poolman suffered back and rib injuries. Not a good day at the office for Lam on his return to his former club at Kingston Park.

But the defeat didn't dampen enthusiasm and the Connacht players knew they were developing into a side that could make a bid for honours, with Harris-Wright outlining the mood in the squad.

"We take it week by week but we definitely have the potential and the players to win a trophy. Even after a

Injury-ravaged Connacht only brought 22 players to play Newcastle Falcons at Kingston Park

Eoghan Masterson is tackled with George Naoupu and Sean O'Brien in support

Jack Carty surveys his options

big defeat we think it's definitely achievable this year.

"It's important that we get our squad back healthy and everyone keeps working hard on our game in the system that we have. It is definitely something that we are looking for," he said.

Ulster came to the Sportsground on St Stephen's Day for the first of the festive derby games. A Paddy Jackson penalty had Ulster 3-0 in front at the break, with AJ MacGinty cancelling that after the restart. But Connacht couldn't prevent a first home defeat of the season when Nick Williams barged over for the only try of the contest late in the game to seal a 10-3 win in front of 5,876 people, the biggest crowd of the season at the Sportsground.

It was a disappointing way to finish 2015 but Kieran Marmion, back for his first game after

injury, was looking forward to the New Year's Day clash with Leinster at the RDS.

"Obviously it was a disappointing result against Ulster. It was tough after the three weeks out but it was good to get 80 minutes under my belt.

"We just need to be more clinical against Leinster. Like what we did against Ulster, but make sure that we are accurate with all of the stuff like passing and kicking. We need to take the opportunities when they come," said Marmion.

At least there were no new injuries for Lam to be worried about, but he knew an improvement was needed if they were to get what would be only Connacht's second ever win in Dublin in the professional era.

"There is so much that we can take forward to this week, one of the areas we need to improve is particularly around our set-piece detail. A couple of roles, people weren't in the right places," said Lam.

Ultan Dillane evades the grips of Ulster's Luke Marshall

CHAPTER ELEVEN
Survival

Michael Bradley spent seven years as head coach in Connacht, battling inadequate budgets, poor facilities, some horrid results and the constant poaching of players. Other than that, he really enjoyed it!

He didn't have the emotional attachment to the province as he was from Cork, but he wasn't long becoming as committed as any native and he stuck with it, year after year, until he handed over the reins to his protégé Eric Elwood.

He has great admiration for former CEO Gerry Kelly, team manager Tim Allnutt, Elwood and many more who kept the show on the road through so many frustrating and difficult years.

But, for the former Irish captain, two men stood out – men who epitomised all that Connacht stood for. To him, John Holland and Mick Grealish summed up everything that was worthwhile in the province.

Holland was the groundsman at the Sportsground for many years, a role his father Tom also carried out, and a job that is now being done by John's son David. Three generations of the same family, who lived across the road from the entrance to the Sportsground, serving Connacht rugby.

The family aspect of their commitment was matched on the field in December 2001 when Ted Robinson made his debut for the province, following in the footsteps of his father Frank and his grandfather, former Galway mayor Josie Owens, as the only third generation player for Connacht.

Mick Grealish, whose many roles range from match steward, to chairman of the branch's stadium committee, to Connacht president in 2008-09, was involved in Our Lady's Boys Club all his life.

Holland and Grealish grew up in the city around the same time and both spent their working lives with the Electricity Supply Board (ESB). But they were never far from the Sportsground and never far away when there was work to be done.

"Sometimes I would go in very early in the morning and the first person I'd meet would be Johnny Holland. And you might leave late that night and you'd meet him again on the way out. And in between you might bump into Mick Grealish several times during the day. They were always doing stuff, always working and planning,

and they just had such a great way about them. Players, everyone, loved them, they have such a great way with people.

"My personal opinion is that if you didn't have people like that in the club, you wouldn't have a club. You need the Johnny Hollands and the Mick Grealishs. Johnny Holland's family story is a fantastic story, so too is Mick Grealish's. And their stories should be told to everyone who comes to Connacht. Not necessarily that Connacht won the league in 2016, but that these people exist and it's them that you're playing for," said Bradley.

The former Irish scrum-half said he was thrilled that the supporters who stuck with the team over the difficult years finally got to taste success.

"You go back to those days when there were 600 people or less watching a match. They're the heroes. You wouldn't miss one person in 6,000. You wouldn't miss 20 or 30 people but you would in 600. Every second week, in horrible difficult conditions, bad facilities."

Connacht made progress, season on season, but never at a sufficient rate to keep up with most of their opponents and with their status still unclear, any of the talented players that they unearthed were ripe for picking by the other provinces.

In some cases it was argued that players were just returning home to their native province after getting game-time with Connacht, but this argument was often flawed.

It was one thing when Kerryman John O'Sullivan went to Munster, but another thing when Paul Warwick, who couldn't qualify for Ireland because he had played sevens for his native Australia, was poached by them.

Similarly, Fionn Carr's return to Leinster was understandable but the two players he arrived in Galway with in 2008 went in opposite directions when all three left in 2011. Limerick native Sean Cronin went to Leinster and Dubliner Ian Keatley was signed by Munster.

"They were tough years, from 2003 onwards," said Billy Glynn. "We were just struggling on. And the union still wanted to get rid of us, but were now afraid to do so. The IRFU was now doing well financially, so they could afford Connacht, but there was never any love lost. They

Adrian Flavin lets off some steam against Newcastle Falcons in the Challenge Cup in 2007

HIGH-FLYERS...Gavin Duffy is tackled by Doug Howlett in 2009

SNOWMAN...Keith Matthews peers through the snow versus Harlequins in 2010

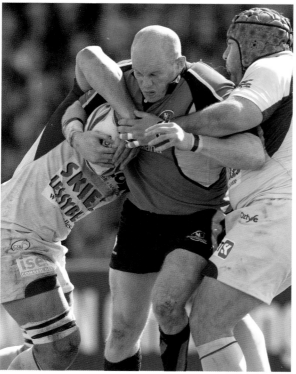

TACKLE...Johnny O'Connor gets stuck in to Bourgoin in 2010

AUSSIE BOYS...Paul Warwick is embraced by Andrew Farley in 2004 following a win over Narbonne in Europe

just gave what they had to and nothing more. Enough to keep it going but not enough to make up the ground on the others."

Bradley was joined on the coaching staff by Eric Elwood when he retired from playing in 2005, with most of the notable victories coming in Europe, reaching the Challenge Cup quarter-finals four times and the semi-finals twice in a six-year spell to 2010.

The limited playing resources meant that Connacht had to target games and it made sense to keep players in reserve for when they were playing the other Irish provinces in particular.

That led to some unusual results. For example, in September 2008 Connacht were hammered 58-0 away to Cardiff Blues. A week later, with a full strength side, they defeated Leinster 19-18.

"I remember Gerry Kelly came into the dressing room after the away Cardiff game," said Michael Swift. "He was pissed off and said it just wasn't good enough. It was in the Arms Park, it was in the tiny dressing room and you know things aren't good when the chief executive has to do that. But we went out and won the following week.

"More often than not we seemed to have good starts. Then during international periods we didn't have many players going away, but these days, thankfully that has changed. Looking back on results the league was never our favourite area. But we could always put together a run in Europe.

"In 2010, for example, we got to the Challenge Cup semi-final, beat Bourgoin in the quarter-final and lost to Toulon, but in the league we were awful. It highlighted the lack of strength we had in our squad. We had a strong 15, or maybe 23, but with injuries there wasn't much coming through. But it's a hard balancing act when you have limited resources."

A big breakthrough was achieved when negotiations were successfully completed to bring Johnny O'Connor home from Wasps and Gavin Duffy from Harlequins in 2007.

"I think that was the time when we just got a little bit of breathing space," said Bradley. "Just a little bit, and that's all it was. It helped conversations with other players: 'There's a future here and there's a positive future.' Getting the two lads home was significant."

But the biggest development was off the field with the building of the gym at the Sportsground. Players saw this as a huge development, a real asset for them. The stadium committee, headed up by Mick Grealish, drove this project while the fitness coaches, Des Ryan and Kevin Cradock were key to its design and the equipment purchased for it.

Both Ryan and Cradock had travelled throughout the world in their own time, looking at facilities at clubs such as Manchester United, Arsenal, ACT Brumbies, Queensland Reds, Blue Bulls, Natal Sharks and Wigan Athletic, and developed a state of the art facility at the Sportsground. The players had been working in small groups in a 50 square metre gym – now they had a 700 square metre facility which was unmatched by any of the other provinces or, indeed, most of the teams they were playing in the league or in Europe.

The facility, which opened in late 2008, was developed using Lottery and other funds.

"I thought the building of the gym was massive," added Bradley. "That was a phenomenal project. Kevin and Dessie did so much to develop that. So, too, did so many others in Connacht. It was their project. All of a sudden, we're training onsite in the gym. We're training onsite on the pitch and we're playing onsite. It brought Connacht to a new level and it was Connacht men who did it all."

The players were particularly chuffed that they had been given priority over other proposed projects aimed at supporters or the corporate sector.

Michael Swift said that the boost the new gym gave was immense and really boosted player morale.

"That was a brave call to make, to actually focus on the playing side first as opposed to the supporters or corporates. To get that gym built and the 30-metre track downstairs, you could see the benefits straight away.

"It was brilliant to be able to do lineout sessions indoors. You could get quality reps done as opposed to working in a wardrobe, basically. You had to split into five groups because there were just two bench-press machines in the old gym. The new gym was to benefit everyone for years and it contributed to winning the league."

Connacht gym

The facility-sharing arrangement with the Irish Greyhound Board, who are the primary tenants at the Sportsground, was often an uneasy relationship at ground level, especially during the week when dog owners would arrive for trials while Connacht were training.

The parking of cars and trailers was haphazard, while the dogs defecated all over the place and was rarely cleaned up by the owners, and this led to friction between players, management and the dog owners.

The sometimes complicated nature of the tenancy meant that Connacht could legally only open a bar if there was greyhound racing on so, in April 2004, when they took on Harlequins in their biggest game ever, the semi-final of the European Challenge Cup, it had to be arranged for two greyhounds to race that Sunday morning in 'a trial' in order for the bar to be opened.

Andrew Farley, normally the most placid individual, still gets agitated when he recalls those days when they were trying to train and the greyhounds were defecating in the car park and on the pitch.

"It was so frustrating. The dogs just shat all over the field. You had guys literally walking their dogs across the field shitting. And us saying to them: 'Can you not shit your dog there?' But they just carried on.

"I had the new gym in my last year and it was a huge turning point. And the same with the synthetic pitch in the area behind the clubhouse.

"I'm so happy for Connacht and where they are. Just to have a stadium to shelter the supporters from the rain and a synthetic pitch to do some lineouts and stuff, where you don't have mud up to your knees.

"I remember at the time, we'd ask for small things and it was during the boom in Ireland. There were construction companies making millions. I couldn't understand how we couldn't get more funding. But we didn't have a marketing or commercial department, and I

see how they operate here now in Grenoble and it is so different. They are ruthless.

"It was starved in Connacht. I'm not saying it's anyway the fault of Connacht or the Irish rugby union, I don't know where it lies. But it was starved, they were hungry."

Peter Bracken revelled in the new gym and saw its opening as a huge step forward, not least as he had seen when Connacht had to improvise with training equipment.

"I remember one day when Steph Nel was the coach. We were doing a rucking drill and we weren't low enough coming into the rucks. So Steph put a rope across between the two goalposts. It was nearly like a Limbo dance to get under the rope. Someone went to ground and we all had to ruck under the rope to clear it out, but of course we all ran full bore in and Swifty hit the ruck slightly high the first time, pretty much clotheslined himself. He nearly got decapitated by the rope! He went in lower the next time, so it worked! I think he never went in high to a ruck ever again."

While the playing roster continued to have a high turnover each season, a lot of constants remained in place and the development of Connacht in the professional era has been helped by having minimal disruption in several off-field areas.

Four kitmen have taken care of Connacht in the professional era and that has contributed hugely to continuity. Outside of the coach, the bagman is possibly the most important appointment. A bagman has never won a trophy for a side, but few teams have been successful without having the right person in that job.

The function extends way beyond sorting out the gear and the logistics. Often the bagman is the link between players and the manager and coach, as well as being the glue for a lot of other departments. There is an agony aunt role to the job, but having the right guy there ensures a lot of harmony.

Mick Grealish and Rodney Ah You

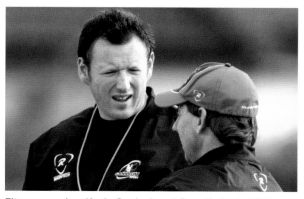

Fitness coaches Kevin Cradock and Greg Muller in 2009

GENERATION GAME...Former groundsman John Holland and his son Dave who now looks after the Sportsground pitch

Seamus King looked after the role in the Warren Gatland years, Tom Newell did the job under Steph Nel, while Fergus Lynch carried out the functions in the Michael Bradley era, before Martin Joyce came on board in 2009.

There has been similar consistency with the team doctor role, with three men looking after that function for most of the professional era. Dr Padraig Sheeran, Dean of the Faculty of Sports and Exercise Medicine, Dr John O'Donnell, who heads up the Emergency Department at University Hospital Galway, and Dr Donal 'Ginger' O'Beirne, who runs a GP practice in the city, looked after the team over the years.

Similarly, a handful of physiotherapists have taken care of the team. Brian Downey was Connacht's first full-time physio when he joined in 2002 and since then the likes of Gavin Malouf, David Hanly, Keith Fox and Garret Coughlan have taken on the task.

The low turnover in these positions created stability, while another area where Connacht benefited hugely over the years was with hotel partners. The Radisson SAS, under general manager Mike de Haast, was a huge supporter, while in more recent times Shay Livingstone in the aptly named Connacht Hotel has provided incalculable backing in the provision of meals,

meeting rooms, accommodation, fitness and other facilities.

All of these factors combined to ensure that while life on the field could be hit-or-miss, off it there was a certain degree of stability. But the development of the new gym is regarded by most as a key moment.

"It was a huge development," recalls Fionn Carr. "Prior to that gym, I remember we were using the Galway footballers' gym for a bit out in Loughgeorge. We were using Galway City Gym and we were also using that small room in Connacht branch headquarters.

"Mick Grealish was very involved. He's a great character. If there was ever a person from Connacht that really was literally lifting Connacht, it was him.

"We will never forget him putting the hay on the pitch one time it was frozen. He'd be the first fella to send you a text message congratulating you if you did something. Even when I was at Leinster, he used to send text messages and I know he does the same for a lot of other lads who moved on.

"John Holland was another who was always around and you see it with his son Dave now as well. They are real Connacht people, a welcome for you when you arrive and they never forget anyone when they leave. Super guys," said Carr.

CHAPTER TWELVE
January 2016

DIARY

Connacht's most glorious year began with them failing to score in a match for the only time in Pat Lam's first three seasons in charge. A 13-0 loss to Leinster in the RDS gave little indication of the better days that were coming down the tracks.

Connacht headed to Dublin with genuine hopes of winning for the first time in six visits to the RDS and Nathan White, a Heineken Cup winner in his sole season with Leinster in 2011-12, reckoned they were in with a good shout.

He was hoping to build on a memorable 2015 that saw him finally make his Irish debut before going on to feature in each of the five games at the World Cup. He went on to play in all of the Six Nations matches but by the following September his career was over due to concussion.

That was the last thing on his mind as he prepared for the trip to the RDS, buoyed by the fervour of the emerging players coming into the side.

"It's a great challenge to go to Dublin but we have a good group of young guys who are pretty enthusiastic about it all. They are bouncing around and that drives the older guys on."

White dismissed Leinster's poor results in the Champions Cup and noted that Leo Cullen's men had chalked up their fifth successive Pro12 win by beating Munster 24-7 in the lead up to this contest.

"I don't think it's really a demise, they played a Toulon team that's pretty handy. And they were only losing by a few points.

"They don't become a bad team overnight, they have got class players. I still think it's a pretty tough ask to go and beat them in Dublin," warned White.

It didn't get any easier for Connacht the following week as they headed for Llanelli looking for their first win at Parc y Scarlets in their eighth visit since the Welsh side moved from Stradey Park.

The derby defeats had knocked Connacht to fourth in the table but experienced hooker Tom McCartney, in his second campaign since joining from the Blues, said they needed to be able to deal with set-backs.

"Obviously it's good to have momentum and to be winning games, but no one's panicking in the camp or anything like that. We definitely back ourselves to go to Scarlets and get a result.

"It is just about going back to process, look at the game to see what we did well and what we could have done a bit better, then to build into the next game.

"There is a busy month ahead. We have had a couple of losses but you just have got to pinch yourself. It is such a long way to go in the season that you just can't get bogged down with results like that and instead, we need to build on to the next week.

"Against Scarlets there are five points up for grabs and if we are good enough then we can go and get them," said McCartney.

It turned out to be a heart-breaker game for Connacht, who were pipped 21-19 when Steven Shingler landed a last minute penalty.

There were high hopes that in a season where they had won for the first time at the Liberty Stadium and Thomond Park, that they would complete the hat-trick and get Parc y Scarlets off the list of bogey grounds – and it looked good early on, despite losing Andrew Browne for the next couple of months to an AC fracture.

A try by Matt Healy and two strikes from the boot of Craig Ronaldson saw Connacht lead 10-3 at the break. Another penalty from Ronaldson and two from Jack Carty in response to a Michael Collins try had the visitors in front going into the closing moments, before Shingler snatched it to keep Scarlets top of the pile.

"We made a lot of improvements, particularly around our attack," said Lam. "We fixed things that weren't quite right about the Leinster and Ulster games.

"We had lots of opportunities that we didn't take. A couple of guys just didn't play by the system.

"But the focus is not on the outcome, it's on the process: how to win games and how this might have affected us here. How we didn't nail this. The positive side is how much improvement we have made over the

> *There were high hopes that in a season where they had won for the first time at the Liberty Stadium and Thomond Park, that they would complete the hat-trick and get Parc y Scarlets off the list of bogey grounds.*

TOP SECRET...
Bundee Aki has a word against Leinster

Team huddle against Leinster

last few weeks," added Lam.

The young players coming through from the academy continued to impress and give great hope for the future. Galway native Sean O'Brien, who turned 21 a few weeks earlier, said the pathway was clearly outlined to aspiring players.

"Pat has given great opportunities to young lads. It's obvious to us there that if we are working hard enough and we are performing that we will get our chance. It's great for all the young lads coming through, it gives you great impetus.

"It is a good sign for Connacht that there are a lot of young lads coming through that we will try and develop over the next few years. We all sat down at the beginning of the year with Pat and we laid out our goals. Mine was that I wanted to be a regular starter.

"I'm still not there, but I am working towards it. Hopefully I can perform well enough to end up there by the end of the year," said O'Brien.

Connacht went back into action in the European Challenge Cup when they travelled to Brive, but there was more late heartbreak in store, and a fifth defeat in a row in all competitions.

Connacht were hoping to win in France for the 12th time and make Brive the latest side they had beaten in

their own backyard, after the wins over Bordeaux-Bègles, Mont-de-Marsan, Béziers, Narbonne, Grenoble, Montpellier (twice), Dax, Bayonne, Toulouse and La Rochelle down the years.

Rory Parata's good strike rate in Europe continued with another try, this time after just 40 seconds, but the boot of Thomas Laranjeira had Brive 9-5 ahead at the break.

John Muldoon crossed for a try, converted by AJ MacGinty, to give Connacht a 13-12 lead and after Laranjeira landed two more penalties, Muldoon struck for his second try to tie the game two minutes from the end. Jack Carty was unable to convert and it seemed that Connacht were poised for their first ever draw in 110 games in the European Challenge Cup.

But then they coughed up a penalty in the final play and Laranjeira landed the match-winner from distance.

"It was probably our worst performance this season," said Lam. "We didn't exit well, we didn't kick well, we made mistakes and off the back of mistakes then we were penalised.

"Ill-discipline gave them easy points. It was just a game that we threw away really, it's extremely disappointing.

"We have just got to play better, that's the main priority

whatever the outcome is against Enisei-STM. But the performance was way below what Connacht should be producing.

"It's obviously an extremely disappointed changing room and so it should be. We are all not happy with that.

"I am expecting a backlash from this performance because, taking the outcome out of it, I am just not happy with the performance whatsoever," he added, at the end of a game which saw Jason Harris-Wright suffer a concussion.

Five defeats on the trot had put a big dent in Connacht's league and European aspirations but with home games to come against Enisei-STM in the Challenge Cup and Scarlets in the Pro12, they had their fate in their own hands and No. 8 Eoghan Masterson said they intended to make the most of it.

"Over the next two weeks, if we get two wins our season is right back on track. That is what we are looking to do, you can't focus on results too much.

"You have to focus on the performance, starting against Enisei, which is going to be a tough physical battle. But we are looking forward to being back at home.

"We have a lot of away games recently so it will be nice to get back out in front of the fans and hopefully they will spur us on and give us a good performance," said the Portlaoise native.

The Russians were no match for Connacht at the Sportsground and tries from Tiernan O'Halloran, Matt Healy, Denis Buckley and Danie Poolman had them 25-0 in front at the break.

Four more tries followed after the restart with Robbie Henshaw, Tom McCartney, Healy and Caolin Blade crossing for scores to secure a quarter-final spot.

That set them up nicely for a second clash in three weeks with Scarlets and with Lam rallying supporters to play their part, a crowd of 5,292 turned up and roared them home to a 30-17 victory which got their campaign right back on track.

"Personally, I still get goose bumps when I walk over from the Clan to the main stand for kick-off. The Sportsground is massive for us and what makes the ground so special is the supporters and the atmosphere they create. It really makes a huge difference to the team.

"There is so much pride in representing Connacht and we can feel the support when we're meeting people in Galway during the week. We really appreciate it," said Lam, as the first day of spring beckoned with them fourth in the table.

Connacht concede the penalty which handed Brive a last gasp victory in France

John Muldoon offloads

Jake Heenan celebrates

Denis Buckley leads the maul through Scarlets at the Sportsground

CHAPTER THIRTEEN
Captain Fantastic

The man who introduced John Muldoon to rugby will never forget the day when it became apparent that the youngster had huge potential. Of course, anyone who has ever broken a rib tends not to forget it in a hurry, and if it so happens that you are a teacher and the guy smashing your ribcage is one of your fired-up students, then it tends to live even longer in the memory.

Daithí Frawley wept when he saw Muldoon going up to collect the Pro12 trophy in Murrayfield but he still gets a chuckle out of the day when his student in Portumna first cut loose on a rugby pitch, even if it left him with a pain in his chest for some time.

"We were at school training and practicing attacking the opposition lineout, when once you tapped the ball the lineout was over. There was no lifting in those days. I got one of the lads to throw in the ball and I filled in as the opposition scrum-half.

"John was to find a gap in the opposition lineout and go through it and hit the scrum-half with everything he had. He took it literally, ploughed through and broke my rib. He was 16 at that stage."

Frawley, a hardy loosehead prop in his day, winced with the pain but didn't realise the extent of the damage, and obviously didn't want Muldoon to know.

"He didn't know, I didn't know myself and it was only a couple of days after that I realised the damage that had been done."

Frawley said it wouldn't be in Muldoon's nature to be nasty, he just went out and gave it everything, a trait that was present on and off the field from a young age.

"John is a gentleman, always was. He never got into trouble, he was a model student. He would have been an example to any anybody and a credit to his parents."

John and Claire Muldoon raised their family in Gortanumera, a remarkable townland six kilometres from Portumna. The Muldoons have been farming there down through the decades. John's mum, Claire, is from Cappataggle, about 25 kilometres away. Claire's sister, Una, and her husband, Pat McDonagh, own the Supermac's franchise and have been the main sponsors of Galway GAA for decades, in addition to sponsoring a host of other sports and events.

A few fields away from the Muldoons are the Cannings while also nearby are the Hayes', two of Galway's most famous hurling families.

They joined forces with a few more families, such as the Treacys and the Smiths, and Portumna, who never won a Galway senior hurling title until 2003, went on to become the dominant club hurling force in the country, winning four All-Ireland club titles in a glorious decade where they picked up six county titles, playing an exhilarating brand of hurling on the way.

Muldoon, who won an All-Ireland minor hurling medal with Galway in 2000, overcoming a Cork side containing future Munster and Ireland scrum-half Tomás O'Leary, would surely have been part of those wins had he not decided to concentrate on rugby.

Indeed, as the glory years dawned for Portumna on the hurling front, you would have got some odds on John Muldoon winning a medal with Connacht before his neighbours, decorated All-Stars Ollie and Joe Canning, would win an All-Ireland medal with Galway.

Joe Canning also toyed with rugby and Shannon RFC, the most prolific winners of the All-Ireland League, tried to sign him. He contemplated following Muldoon's example, but ultimately opted to stay with hurling.

"I played a lot underage in school in Portumna, and then with Ballinasloe as well for a number of years. We won a lot of U-16s, U-18s, U-14s at Ballinasloe," said Canning.

"Daithí Frawley and James Coughlan were the coaches in Portumna, then we had Noel Mannion and Pat Finn in Ballinasloe. They were great.

"When I moved to Limerick for college I was asked to play with Shannon, but I don't know, it was just around the time that we were getting successful with the club. We were just starting, we had just won a club All-Ireland, the hurling was going well at the time."

Canning has followed Muldoon's career and rejoiced in the success of his neighbour, who is six years older

> *Joe Canning also toyed with rugby and Shannon RFC, the most prolific winners of the All-Ireland League, tried to sign him. He contemplated following Muldoon's example, but ultimately opted to stay with hurling.*

SPEEDSTER...Matt Healy takes off down the wing

if they want to be where we are at this time in the season.

"But we also understand that it's early days. There are eight games left and it's the business end the season. We are delighted where we are after we came from," said Healy.

Lam also issued a warning about paying too much heed to the league table in February, as they prepared to head to Parma to take on a Zebre side locked in a battle at the bottom of the table with Treviso for the Italian Champions Cup spot.

"There's still a long way to go. If you get caught looking at the table too much and you take your eye off what your job is, then it doesn't do you any good. We just have got to take it one game a time. We are in a good position, it is good to be where we are. But you can't get too far ahead of yourself.

"It's very interesting, it's very tight. With the World Cup and then when it gets into Six Nations, it levels things out a little bit more as well.

"It's enjoyable to be a part of. We just need to keep doing our job and winning. If you take your eye off the ball and you have a couple of slip-ups, it's so tight up there that you can slip down very quickly," said Lam.

Conceding 34 points to Zebre, the most they ever leaked against an Italian side, was hardly part of the plan but a hat-trick from flying winger Healy was key to them romping home by 51-34.

Niyi Adeolokun got a brace of tries and Kieran Marmion also crossed as Connacht chalked up their biggest scoring tally away from home.

But the injury jinx hit again and Eoghan Masterson's season was finished by a serious knee injury.

The Ospreys were next to come to Galway and city native Eoin McKeon knew that supporters were beginning to hope after three bonus-point wins in a row that this could be a very special season, not just with automatic Champions Cup qualification but also with the possibility of silverware for the first time in history.

"We do have a chance of winning something. We won't get ahead of ourselves. We set our goal of top six in the Pro12, so we can qualify for the higher competition next year.

"It is still early days, but it will be a nice cherry on top of a good season, if we do come away with some silverware," said McKeon.

Connacht were scoring from all angles and the fastest man in the squad, Nigerian-born but Dublin-raised Niyi Adeolokun, was confident that their mid-season slump was behind them.

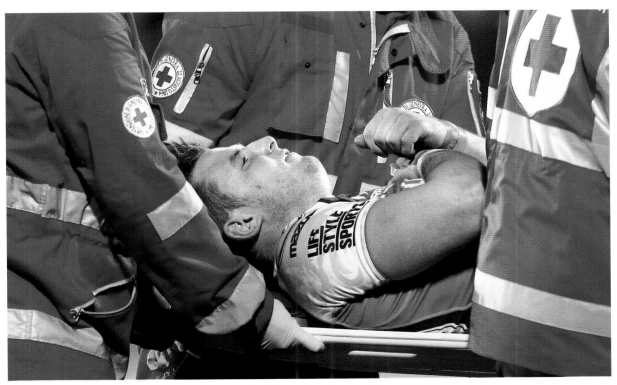

HEARTACHE...Eoghan Masterson's season ends after injury in the win over Zebre in Parma

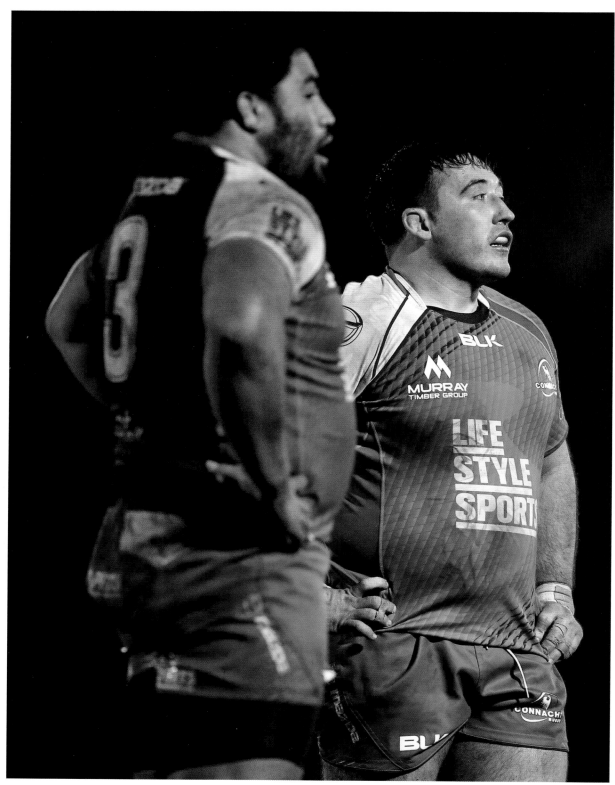

PROPPED UP...Rodney Ah You and Denis Buckley draw breath

"As a team we started the season very well. We were delighted with the way it went. But after that the last month hasn't been great, mainly due to injuries and that. Hopefully now we can pick it up from where we left off when the lads got injured and start winning again."

Adeolokun was just the latest player to have his rugby career re-ignited by Connacht. He was cut from Leinster at U-19 level and was playing soccer for Shelbourne U-20s when he got the opportunity to play for Trinity College, and that's where he came on Connacht's radar less than two years earlier.

"I feel like I have come up a long way since I joined Connacht. I feel like my running lines are a lot better now, and I am much more solid when I am competing in the air.

"I changed my defence as well, with Andre Bell we talk about this stuff. My kicking game has come up a long way because we kick a lot during practice. I feel like my game has really improved but I definitely still have a lot to work on.

"Overall I am better able to read the game and connect better with the guys inside me. Being able to work effectively, makes it more natural with the rest of the backline and it flows better," he said.

Adeolokun wasn't among the try scorers this time as Connacht completed only their second ever double over the Ospreys with tries from Bundee Aki, AJ MacGinty and Matt Healy seeing them home on a day when Craig Ronaldson hit 15 points off the tee. Another concussion for Ben Marshall would rule him out for the remainder of the season though, a low point from a memorable victory.

The win kept Connacht on top of the table going into March and Lam was determined they would set the agenda from here.

"The way we see it, we are at the top. So we put the pressure on everyone else. You either feel the pressure or you apply the pressure.

"We talked about it, one of the main reasons we want the outcome is for top six, but also we are running out of games. Everyone is running out of games and they have got to catch us.

"We know the only way we can do that is by putting the pressure on, by getting the outcome. The only way we do that is to go back to what we have been doing right from pre-season," said Lam.

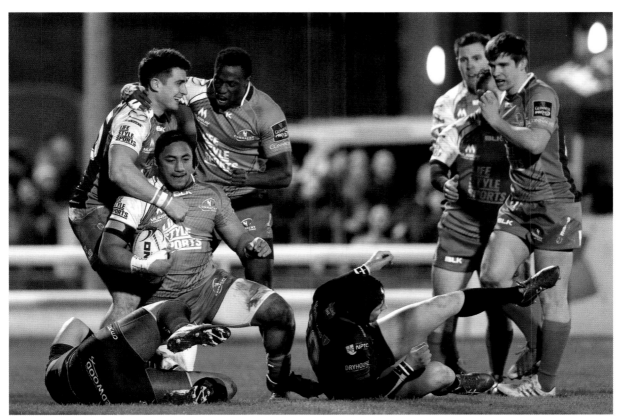

TRY AND TRY AGAIN...Bundee Aki enjoys scoring his side's first try against Ospreys

CHAPTER FIFTEEN
▬Trouble Again

So, to all the Connacht supporters, hands up those of you who have heard of Morgan Buckley? Now, both of you down the back, keep your hands in the air if you can explain how he contributed more to Connacht winning the Pro12 title in Murrayfield than, say, Pat Lam or John Muldoon, or anyone else for that matter. Uh? Morgan who?

It's presumed by most supporters that the closest Connacht came to being disbanded was in 2003 but, in fact, the biggest threat came six years later. On that occasion, staging a march to the IRFU headquarters or conducting any other protest would probably not have saved the province's professional team.

The endless cycle of losing matches and losing money had taken as much toll on those in Connacht as it had in the IRFU. The union kept funding Connacht but couldn't see any return from what seemed to be a bottomless pit.

Connacht's contention was that it wasn't being funded enough for it to go out and make money. Supporters wouldn't come to see a team that was not winning and in order for them to win, funding was needed to invest in players. It was a vicious circle but as the economic downturn hit, both parties had endured enough. Something needed to be done, once and for all.

Both the IRFU and Connacht went into the procedure with the genuine intention of finding a solution, but there were some within the union hoping that this would be the process which would finally see the demise of Connacht, while there were several people running the game in the province who could not see themselves surviving a forensic investigation.

The examination went on for several months. Players, coaches, staff and officers were interviewed; accounts were scrutinised, minutes of meetings examined, stakeholders interviewed, facilities audited, while the IRFU input was also thoroughly checked. Every aspect of Connacht was looked at.

The lengthy report detailed all of this but, essentially, it came down to two things. Connacht financially, in terms of return on investment, was a disaster, and in most other business environments would be closed. However from a rugby potential, there was a glimmer of hope. A potential gem had been spotted and the man who

played God with Connacht, Morgan Buckley, recommended that this be given a chance and that life be breathed into it.

Buckley is from Cork and still lives in Kinsale. He now works for World Rugby as its development general manager, travelling all over the world developing and implementing rugby programmes in 130 member unions.

But, for over a decade and a half, before he took up his current position in 2010, Buckley was one of the most influential people in Irish sport.

Operating under the radar with a low profile, he carried out extensive work for the Irish Sports Council, delving into up to 70 sports, while the IRFU made extensive use of his talents in all four provinces and nationally in the domestic and professional games.

Buckley graduated as a physiotherapist from Trinity College before moving to New Zealand, where he did a Masters in sports management in the early 1990s and then worked in their domestic sports industry for several years. He worked with Steve Tew, the current New Zealand rugby chief executive, when Tew was in the sports council there. Buckley's work with a sports management company included projects in Australia in the lead up to the 2000 Olympics, but in 1996 he came back to Ireland and helped John Treacy with the strategy that led to the formation of the Irish Sports Council.

He was project manager of the sports strategy group that conducted the first ever full review of sports in Ireland and looked at the whole long-term plan for sport in the country. A key part of that was the establishment of a Department of Sport, headed by a full minister at the cabinet table. This was to prove critical for Irish rugby, among others, in light of the investment and development plans that were subsequently launched.

Buckley did a lot of work with the International Rugby Board, as World Rugby was then known, after returning to Ireland. He developed restructuring plans in Canada and the United States, while extensive work in Argentina led to a restructuring of rugby in that country, where he project-managed their subsequent entry into the Rugby Championship.

In Ireland, Buckley worked with all of the Olympic sports, particularly sailing, rowing, boxing and athletics, and when the IRFU came calling in 2008, asking him to

examine Connacht, it was one of the final jobs he took on before taking up his current position with World Rugby.

Buckley knew Irish rugby inside out by that stage, having started his first project in the mid-1990s while the IRFU tried to prepare for professionalism.

"In those days Irish rugby received no funding from government. They had been cut off since they toured South Africa in the apartheid era and that had never been restored. The IRFU were never really too bothered about it because there wasn't a whole pile of funding going.

"Then in the mid-90s, as the game was turning professional, the whole model for Irish rugby had to change and change rapidly. So I was appointed by the IRFU to do the first benchmarking review of Irish rugby because there was no strategic plan.

"We did the benchmarking and that led to the first instruction of the IRFU to create a management committee. There was only the full council as such before that."

The IRFU were sufficiently well-resourced to run the game while it was amateur, but this needed to change rapidly with the advent of the professional era. There were very few employees, there was a huge volunteer culture and it was poorly set up to embrace the professional game. Ireland lagged behind other countries.

A benchmarking exercise, initially used in New Zealand, was applied to Ireland's national team, examining the win rate.

"I think it was about 28 per cent. Against the top countries it was about 15 per cent. By that it meant that Ireland won only 28 per cent of matches played. People knew that it was low but they were shocked when they realised how far off the pace they were," said Buckley.

"There were some very big decisions taken. In '99 Argentina beat Ireland and we were having one of our strategic planning meetings the day after that. It was like being at a funeral, it was the first time Ireland hadn't qualified (automatically) for a World Cup and they were all going: 'we can't let that happen again'. Basically it was agreed that more resources needed to be put into a high performance system."

The work of Dr Liam Hennessy, the IRFU's national fitness director, was crucial. He could see the need to limit the number of games each player took part in, for proper pre-season training regimes, and for the alignment of the demands of playing for the provinces and the national team. Basically, all sides needed to sing

SAVIOUR ...World Rugby's development manager Morgan Buckley, who spotted the hidden potential in Connacht

off the same hymn sheet.

"In those days Irish players' strength, fitness and conditioning was miles off the pace," added Buckley.

"We had rugby talent but building people who were fit for purpose needed to be kicked up a gear, and it did under Dr Liam's direction. The win rate goes up from something like 28 per cent in the mid-90s, starts creeping up to 40, 50, 60 and 70 per cent for the 2003 World Cup in Australia. After Argentina they realised that if they didn't invest, they wouldn't remain competitive.

"They had to put in place a system that brought players back. A lot of the players in '99 were playing rugby in the UK and in France. There was hardly any contracting of players. So they had to go to contracting and set up a professional games system here. That cost a huge amount of money and in that period immediately after '99, up to 2003, they laid down the real foundations for a professional game model."

That was, of course, when the first threat to disband Connacht came into the public domain, as the IRFU examined the best structure to take the game forward.

"My view, working closely with the IRFU, was that whenever a big decision had to be made, they all took the right decision. They weren't always the fastest at making those big decisions, which in many ways was a real strength. They based their decisions on hard analysis and an understanding of what business they were in; what were the key ingredients.

"They realised that our model was closest to Australia. They had to compete with other sports – in those days there were 28,000 – 30,000 players in the country. They had to build a domestic game model because they couldn't import players, and continue to resource it. In those days the expenditure from the clubs in the All-Ireland League was significant."

The IRFU realised that they needed to spend serious money developing their venues if they were to generate the cash needed to fund the professional game – not just redeveloping Lansdowne Road but also the provincial grounds.

"They talked about building proper stadia because that is the engine room for generating the cash. You had to have competitive teams to play in the stadia, but if you have the teams but not the stadia, the money doesn't come.

"There was a continual drain on the resources. That led to the first strategic plan and in the middle of that planning process, there was a funding crisis. They looked carefully at the resources available and thought how they were going to keep five big ships afloat. They had the national team, and they had the four provincial teams.

"In those days the provincial teams weren't generating the revenues needed to keep their head above water. They had to be subsidised, to the tune of probably 100 per cent to start with, then 80 per cent, 70 per cent and so on. The Leinsters, Ulsters and Munsters began to contribute 10, 20 and 40 per cent. But Connacht were always in the 80 if not 90 per cent bracket, because they were not generating the revenue to keep themselves going, while costs were rising."

Buckley was project manager on the IRFU strategic plan which was produced in 2003, with the Connacht march taking place while it was being prepared.

"There was intense pressure on the volunteers. And the IRFU didn't want to be cutting down a whole wing of Irish rugby. They were also thinking they could pull the whole show down if they don't have the resources. There is intense competition between the four provinces in Irish rugby – it is the best thing about it – but they also don't give each other any quarter. And then, at the decision-making meetings you still have the reps from the four provinces all arguing their own case for a piece of the pie. There was a business model but also a representational model in the mix of it. All of those are strengths and weaknesses."

The Celtic Tiger, the success by Ireland under Eddie O'Sullivan and Munster finally achieving Heineken Cup success brought about a wonderful period, before Leinster found their path to glory and tapped into the vast cash resources available in Dublin.

But Connacht were continuing to struggle and by 2008, with the recession starting to kick in, Ulster also struggling financially and the IRFU facing a huge bill for the redevelopment of Lansdowne Road (not to mention an uphill battle to sell long-term ticket packages) the union took a fresh look at Connacht to see if it continuing with the project was worthwhile.

"Connacht's business model was struggling because their average home crowd was between 2,000 and 3,000, Leinster were getting between 8,000 and 12,000 at their games, while Munster were always going to get 10,000 and in the big matches it spiked. Connacht benchmarked lowest attendance rate, lowest everything and 90 per cent funding model. So clearly there was something not right, something unsustainable.

"I had also worked with Scottish rugby to look at where they stood. With Murrayfield they had a debt of 22 million on their balance sheet. They initially had four professional teams in mind, then they went to three. Then they took the huge decision to close the Borders down and then they went to two. The people in Irish rugby looked across the pond and said: 'that's not viable for running a competitive international team. Two professional teams is too low a base to run a professional game. Three is struggling, two is really off the charts. Players needed to be playing a minimum of 20 games and a maximum of 24 to be competitive'."

Buckley spent several months looking at every aspect of Connacht and compiled a detailed analysis of the situation, benchmarking everything.

"We put all of the facts on the table so any decision would be based on facts. The big issue was that there was huge emotion from the previous march. There was also a realisation from Connacht that they had gone beyond marching because they knew themselves what the business model looked like.

"The review took about two to three months at the end of 2008. I submitted a report just coming up to Christmas. The key picture that emerged from it was that the IRFU's number one aim is the success of the national team and to have a sustainable national team programme you need to have the base of 120 to 130 professional players, maybe more.

"At any given time, 25 to 30 per cent of those players are injured in the pro game. At any given time each team is allowed six international players max, non-Irish qualified players who are absolutely vital to the success. But four by six is 24 players. And then with your 25 per cent out injured, if you have 100 players and 24 foreign that's 76 to choose from.

"So if you have only got 100 players, which effectively is three squads of 30, your Irish team base comes down to 50 fit players from which to run your international programme. Add another few people that aren't on form and then you are heading into Scotland territory, of trying to run a game with two teams. Very simply, if you go from four to three, at any given time you are going to have in the order of 50 to 60 players that your national coach can select from. There is very little room for error to have a squad. That assumes those 50 players are on form, and it also assumes that we have got depth with those players and the right players are available.

"When you do the maths, Ireland needed four squads of 30 in the professional game, because that gives you the wriggle room to play at the level.

"The next element of the equation was that Connacht had a brilliant academy programme. Nigel Carolan was doing outstanding work. They were ahead of the game in terms of integrating schools and clubs. What he was doing, and we can now see the result of it, was outstanding. You close that down, you then take out all of that out of the pipeline. It's not just a national team

programme, it's the academies that go with it.

"Nigel and these guys said when we interviewed them, what's the point in having an academy if you don't have a professional team above that to play for? Where would the guys in the academy play after that? So now you are also taking out the academy, effectively taking out the whole western seaboard.

"You had a very effective academy programme, taking in home grown players and converting them. Since then it has come into its own and so has Nigel with the Irish U-20s. You could see the value with the winning of the Pro12. If you haven't got an academy you can't have a professional team playing week in, week out, and then the national team falters.

"The rugby argument is saying we need four strong provinces and four strong academies to feed the national objective. When you did the maths with the professional coaches, the CEO, the national coach, they are going wow: 'take a whole team and the job is precarious, numbers wise. You damage the overall rugby model'.

"If you start sliding down, Scotland and Italy will overcome you. And then you have trouble with Namibia and Georgia giving Ireland scares in the World Cup. You could see that come World Cup time, a weakened Irish team would have been easier to knock off. These are threads. You pull that thread and next thing Ireland take a hit against a tier two country who we have never lost to in a World Cup.

"You look at the Argentina model, they now have 12 high performance centres. They are the country that is accelerating player development better than anyone and that is why they did astonishingly well against Ireland in the last World Cup. They have got a big playing population, Super Rugby and 12 high performance centres. So these academies and high performance centres have to be run; they feed the beast and they are vital. In terms of the recommendation to the IRFU I made, it was based on a rugby point of view purely," added Buckley.

The potential lying within the Connacht academy and the need to keep a professional playing roster of around 120-130 players were the key reasons for continuing to fund the province.

But the report also outlined that Connacht needed to be funded accordingly, if it was to achieve these objectives. So, those few people in the IRFU who were hoping for a recommendation for closure, were now being told to they needed to put their hands deeper into their pockets.

Connacht were also being told that they needed to get

their act together and move from a committee-led organisation towards a streamlined business board model.

"The report highlighted the need for massive improvement in the way Connacht was governed, run and operated. It highlighted the need for a professional game board (PGB), for proper decision-making and professional marketing, and that the facilities in Galway weren't fit for purpose. They needed a minimum 4,000 capacity to generate the revenues required. Connacht couldn't rely on an 80–20 model from the IRFU. The report made a recommendation to improve the model, the governance and decision-making.

"There was a mix of best practice rugby, best practice governance, best practice in business, all of that. All parties would have had a lot of discussion on this. The IRFU made the decision that they would invest but there had to be improvement. I suppose all of that came together in May of this year.

"The IRFU are good people who make good rugby decisions and they realised that the rugby decision was the primary one – that the business one had to be made work. The saving grace was the raw material, the potential and ingredients. But it needed a massive shifting in gear.

"I tried to keep it objective. It was purely: 'these are the facts, this is the situation and this is the recommendation I have'. Results were dismal in the Pro12. I highlighted the consequences of closing it down but you couldn't predict the success.

"The report also said there was no guarantee of success but laid bare the consequences of not investing in Connacht, and offered a doomsday scenario.

"That was where the IRFU had to take a punt. Who could have predicted that Pat Lam would come along? From being bottom of the league you would have been a mad man to predict the success. It just shows what can happen if the raw ingredients are there. Nigel and his lads run a bloody good show.

"There were some people there that really cared deeply about rugby in Connacht. They soldiered long and hard and they fought like hell to keep rugby going when it wasn't looking possible at times.

"Once they made the decision, both parties moved quickly. The IRFU accepted the report and that they had to keep it going. But they accepted that the implementation and turnaround was equally important."

Buckley joined the IRB shortly after that but he has watched the way Connacht and the IRFU have developed and believes a lot can be learned from the way the game has developed in this country.

"I work towards developing the game in other parts of the world. But there is a huge amount that can be learned from Irish rugby and how it has succeeded globally.

"I don't reference Connacht but I draw on that experience. I am hugely proud of it."

Buckley managed to watch the Pro12 final on television, having just got home from Africa.

"I had just come from Zimbabwe after attending the World U-20 trophy there. We had our development programmes globally, our new mass participation programme and involved 130 countries around the world. We had training in Africa and then I was in Zimbabwe. The methodologies I would have learned with Irish rugby, I applied in this work.

"I had just got in the door in time to see the match. I was watching it and cheering, it was fantastic.

"But I didn't create that success, it was Pat Lam and the players."

However, it was his recommendation to breathe life into the rugby in Connacht which got them there.

But what would have happened if it wasn't the rugby potential which swayed the argument?

"If you were taking the situation on an accounting decision you would have closed it down."

Morgan Buckley

CHAPTER SIXTEEN
_The Rebirth

The report by Morgan Buckley was the real game-changer for Connacht. Once the IRFU and Connacht agreed to implement the recommendations, neither party wasted any time in putting their plans into action.

The new course being plotted meant more backing from the IRFU for Connacht, not just financially, while the province was tasked with massive improvements in how it was run.

A professional game board (PGB), with both parties nominating three members, was established to oversee the whole project. Jimmy Staunton from Castlebar, who headed up the ownership of Elvery's Sports, was appointed as chairman.

Philip Browne, the chief executive of the IRFU, said that changes were required in order to find a way forward.

"Connacht received additional financial support from the IRFU on a number of occasions (as have other provinces). It became obvious that the structures surrounding the professional game and its management were inadequate for the task, and the province had an inability to live within its means.

"To safeguard further IRFU investment, a new professional game board was set up in the province, with members appointed by the IRFU and also by Connacht Rugby, which reports directly into the IRFU.

"The new PGB has been at the heart of the turnaround, both in financial and rugby terms, and has accepted responsibility and accountability for performances on and off the pitch," he said.

The extra funding and goodwill offered a level of security which Connacht had not enjoyed to this point since the game went professional and, for the first time, real progress was made.

Significant money was directed towards marketing, improvements in spectator facilities were introduced, while on the playing front, contracts were extended and planning could take place for a number of years rather than going from season to season.

"I used to always make the point, you could only plan short term," said former Connacht chief executive Gerry Kelly. "Strategic planning was not possible without clarity.

"But it was accepted that the future of the province

was unclear and there was acceptance by both parties that the status quo could not continue. Both parties agreed that a fully-external review was required with one-year player contracts in the interim."

Kelly and the officers knew that if a recommendation for closure was made by Buckley, then it would be almost impossible to prevent it. Everyone had enough at that stage, it was time to either fund it or finish it.

"I remember Morgan Buckley came and he literally went through everything with a fine comb. He would look at everything as independently as possible. He would have gone through minutes of meetings and everything and looked at facilities.

"And I always remember one day in particular. We had a match and I said to Morgan: 'the supporters are going to pull the plug. How can you expect people to come and watch a match with no cover?'

"He put two options in front of me. One was for Ireland to operate with three professional franchises, and the second was to continue with four professional franchises. He recommended option two strongly with the provision that more support and funding would be given to Connacht. He came out very strong on that. He went through a scenario that if we were down to three, the player succession for the national team would be impacted.

"Connacht would be gone, had he gone with option one. At that stage things were so desperate from both sides," said Kelly.

One of the first things to be done was a detailed study to find what level of interest there was for rugby in Connacht.

"What the research told us, the population of Connacht was about 500,000 at the time. The feedback told us that 67 per cent of them were actually interested in rugby, 31 per cent were very interested. The Galway city figure was 70 per cent.

"The arrival of Heineken Cup rugby for the first time in 2011 was massive, that was a huge driver," added Kelly.

The three-year mandate of the PGB was also reflected in player contracts and now they could be tied down for a few seasons, which allowed Eric Elwood, who had taken over from Michael Bradley at the start of the 2010-11 campaign, to plan his resources on the field

TOP MAN...Eric Elwood took over as head coach in 2010

over more than one campaign.

Putting such an iconic figure in charge of the team greatly assisted the new marketing drive. The marketing budget went from €40,000 to €400,000 in a short time, going from one person to seven people.

An ambitious target of more than doubling the sponsorship to €600,000 was surpassed in the first year, when €820,000 was raised.

Staff, volunteers and players came into the branch headquarters for two nights in a row to drive season ticket sales by telephone. Season tickets went from 550 to 4,000 in two years.

The Clan Stand was built, almost entirely with government funding, and the supporters' club – The Clan – was formed. By the time Toulouse came to town in the Heineken Cup, the ground could hold more than 9,000 people.

The match-day experience was improved with more food and drink outlets, while the venue was dressed up – not an easy task given the layout of the Sportsground.

Connacht changed their mantra from survival to success. The 'Front Up, Rise Up' campaign was instigated to drum up support. Targets were set to produce players for Ireland and to turn the Sportsground into a fortress.

"The strengths were focused management of the team and academy," said Kelly. "In the 2009-10 season, 29 players had represented Ireland at various levels. It's a startling figure, between schools, youths and the others. The high-performing academy was now the top one in Ireland. There were quality training facilities on the same site, they were there at that time. While the PGB did an awful lot, they inherited an awful lot as well. There was a lot in place.

"You were given the money to do it. Plans for the stands and new branding initiatives, to improve the link between supporters and fans, improve merchandising, and so on, were implemented. They were all tackled and funded.

"What's working in Connacht is now being applied everywhere else."

One of the targets set was: 'Connacht will become the most improved team in Europe, committed to a culture of winning through excellence'.

Of course, you could understand if the volunteers who ran Connacht over the years were wondering what they might have achieved if they received such lavish funding and goodwill from the IRFU.

The ultimate irony was that the Connacht brand continued to grow in 2011-12, when the team went on its

Elwood and John Muldoon pictured with the Heineken Cup in 2011

GOOD TIMES...Chief executive Gerry Kelly and Eric Elwood share a happy moment

worst losing run in the professional era, getting turned over 14 games in a row from the end of September to the end of January.

In many ways it illustrated the level of the boost that comes with Heineken Cup qualification. It was Connacht's first season in Europe's premier event and optimism levels soared when they won three of their opening four games in what was then the RaboDirect Pro12, but a 26-21 loss away to Ospreys in the Liberty Stadium saw the wheels come off. Even Treviso came to the Sportsground and won, while the other Italian side, Aironi, beat them in Viadana.

But the supporters stuck with the side and who will ever forget the crescendo which greeted the full-time whistle when they beat Harlequins 9-8 at the Sportsground for their first Heineken Cup win in January 2012.

It was the final pool match, Connacht had lost all five prior to that, but the win was greeted as if they had qualified. All it did was knock Harlequins – coached by Elwood's former teammate Conor O'Shea – out of the competition.

But the win showed that Connacht could compete at this level and what might be achieved if the western province could just get everything to fall into place.

NEW DIRECTION...The inaugural Connacht Professional Game Board 2011 with, from left, IRFU Chairman Finbarr Crowley, Conor McGuinness, Damien Devaney, Liam Rattigan, Pat O'Connor, Jimmy Staunton (Chairman), Simon Heaslip, Steve Cunninghan, Connacht CEO Gerry Kelly and IRFU President John Hussey

The new Clan Stand takes shape in the autumn of 2011

CHAPTER SEVENTEEN
March 2016

DIARY

Connacht may have had only two games in March but this was nonetheless a month that will not be forgotten by fans of the province for a long time.

Both games, away to Edinburgh and home to Leinster, produced superb results – but the highlight of the month was a defining moment for Connacht rugby when five players represented the team on the field for Ireland, for the first time ever.

Robbie Henshaw, Kieran Marmion and Nathan White had already made their bow over the past couple of seasons, while Ultan Dillane got capped against England. Consequently, the arrival off the bench of Finlay Bealham with 14 minutes left in the victory over Italy marked a new line in the sand for the game of rugby in Connacht.

By then Connacht had taken another giant leap towards a semi-final spot with a 28-23 win over Edinburgh at Murrayfield, with many players vowing as they left the field that they would be back there again in May.

One man who was finding the harder ground more to his liking was Bundee Aki and he said they were gearing up for a huge finish to the season.

"The weather is drying up now. Against Ospreys both teams were throwing the ball around and we can only just start getting better from here. You've got to enjoy and embrace that weather. Playing footie in the summer is the best thing ever so you've got to embrace it.

"There's a lot of things that have changed in the Sportsground. Our management have worked really hard on what we need to do on the field. The boys have obviously worked very hard too, and it's paying off. We've just got to keep working hard on the training paddock.

"We are practicing a lot of our off-loading game and boys working hard off the ball. You can see it on the field, boys working for each other. Boys make a half-break, someone is on their shoulder. It's great to see what we're working on, on the training paddock, seeing that on the field."

'You can see it on the field, boys working for each other. Boys make a half-break, someone is on their shoulder. It's great to see what we're working on, on the training paddock, seeing that on the field.'

It was only Connacht's second ever double over Edinburgh in a season and the first time they achieved it since 2003-04.

Converted tries from AJ MacGinty and Jake Heenan had Connacht 14-0 in front at the break, with Aki and Eoin McKeon fending off an Edinburgh revival in the second-half to wrap up the bonus-point win.

An ankle ligament injury saw Craig Ronaldson added to the casualty list, but the performances of the team ensured that those injured on the sidelines couldn't wait to get back.

"It's good to see the lads stepping up and putting in some massive performances both away and at home. It doesn't make it more difficult for me while I'm injured," said lock Ben Marshall.

"It motivates me and it motivates the team and the trainers to keep pushing on.

"You know that the team that I left is in a much better place now. It just pushes me to get better, and to make sure that when I am there that I am doing the best I can.

"These people around me have set the foundations and I need to drive it on, looking towards European rugby next year," he said.

His former side, Leinster, were the next visitors to Galway for a first versus second clash on 26 March, with the Irish internationals back in action for both sides.

A crowd of 7,300 watched an enthralling match where Connacht discipline and their self-belief rose to a new level in a tie where scores were at a premium.

It was a titanic clash between Connacht, the league's top try scorers, and Leinster, with the best defensive record in the competition, going head to head in a cracking contest.

A try from Marmion, converted by MacGinty, resulted in Connacht enjoying a 7-0 interval lead but two penalties from Ian Madigan ensured a nerve-racking finish.

Leinster piled on the pressure in the closing minutes with Connacht refusing to kick when they had the ball, and when a series of five-metre scrums were repelled by

'I CAN FLY'...Bundee Aki scores away to Edinburgh

OVER AND OUT...AJ MacGinty stretches to score as well in Murrayfield

Lam's men, forcing a turnover, the Sportsground exploded as Champions Cup rugby for 2016-17 was all but secured on a 7-6 scoreline.

It was probably the most decisive one-point victory ever achieved by Connacht.

It was the first of three Irish derbies in a row, games which would define their season. But a glance at their record against Leinster, Ulster and Munster in the professional era wouldn't be long dampening optimism.

Prior to the Leinster match, Connacht had played a total of 77 games against the three Irish provinces in the league and up to then they had recorded just 12 victories, two draws and 63 losses.

"We have worked hard to be here and it's important to understand how we got here," said Lam. "It's just fantastic for Connacht, for the whole province. We have

---

'Everyone needs to perform at training, and perform at the weekends if you want to play next week. So that drives a lot of lads to perform, and I think that's been going very well for us this season.'

---

always focused on what we do as a collective. We are not a team of individuals."

Once again Connacht suffered another injury blow with Nathan White going off with a concussion after just six minutes, in what turned out to be his last action on a rugby pitch before he was forced to retire from the game in September.

Next up for Connacht was a trip to Ravenhill on April Fool's Day, a venue where they had not won in 12 visits in the professional era.

Indeed you have to go back to 1960 for their last win there.

The overall record in the league was 21 wins for Ulster, three for Connacht and one draw, but Quinn Roux said that they felt that they were up for the challenges that the business end of the season would present.

"It's going to be a tough couple of weeks coming up but we are well prepared for that. There is a lot of competition in certain positions and that's healthy for the squad.

"Everyone needs to perform at training, and perform at the weekends if you want to play next week. So that drives a lot of lads to perform, and I think that's been going very well for us this season," he said.

LET'S GO!...Bundee Aki throws down the challenge to Leinster's Ben Te'o at the Sportsground

CHAPTER EIGHTEEN
___The Clan

Andrew Farley, like all who went before him and most who came after him, never won anything during the six years he played for Connacht.

So, perhaps it is no surprise that the engraved crystal plate which he received when he was inducted into the Hall of Fame by the Clan, the Connacht supporters' club, is proudly on display in the study of the Grenoble home he shares with his wife Lucy and their three children, Ava, Sophia and Thomas.

Connacht, like a lot of other unsuccessful sides bereft of cup-winning teams to celebrate down through the years, don't have a great record in honouring former players, but that has been remedied somewhat by the Clan, who induct two former players each season into their Hall of Fame. It is just one of the many contributions they make to Connacht rugby, and it has gone down well with supporters and former players.

Farley, perhaps one of Connacht's best ever signings, soldiered in the years immediately after the threat to disband the side but before the IRFU started pumping

money into the organisation, following the establishment of the professional game board.

He was a wonderful addition to the playing roster at the Sportsground, bringing typical Aussie positivity, a trait that made him very popular on and off the field. He arrived in the summer of 2003 and was named captain the following year, a few weeks before his 24th birthday.

He went on to make 109 league and 40 European appearances for Connacht, in addition to featuring in several other games for the province, captaining them for three of his six seasons at the Sportsground.

He returned to the Sportsground in the summer of 2015 for a pre-season friendly with the Grenoble side that he was managing at the time. He saw out his playing career with the Alpine club, captaining them to promotion to the Top 14, and then took over as team manager after they established themselves in the top flight in France.

He hadn't been back to the Sportsground since he left in 2009 and the honour bestowed on him by the Clan

The Connacht Clan on tour

made the return with his new team all the more special.

"The Clan made a presentation, the Hall of Fame, which was excellent. I'd never experienced anything like that before. It meant a huge amount. It was not that Connacht owed me anything but I was loyal and I felt that I gave everything I could possibly give in the six years I'd been there.

"It was more emotional for me when I went back for that friendly match and ironic that it was the start of the same year they won the title. It's funny actually how things come around.

"When I drove into Galway, I think it was just all the memories which made it so special. When you see things, it triggers things in your brain, and all the memories that came back and the changes and the development of the city. It was awesome.

"When you're in the cyclone you don't really see what's happening, but being away for so long and coming back and seeing all the development, it's like revisiting a child. If you don't see your child for a long time, they grow massively but if you see them every day, it's hard to notice that change.

"I was quite emotional. I ran into guys that I was close to, like James Heaslip, Niall Beatty, Eric and guys like that. And guys from outside rugby too that I was mates with, and I saw the old doctor and all that sort of stuff. And looking around the improvements at the club and

stuff like that. That gave me an awesome feeling. I know I didn't do any of it but it was awesome to see the club improve and be in a better place and to have been part of it at one stage."

Farley said that receiving the award from the Clan brought the memories flowing back, the good Challenge Cup campaigns, the infrequent but treasured league wins, and games like the clash against South Africa at the Sportsground when he skippered them against a side warming up for what turned out to be a very successful World Cup campaign in 2007, one which saw them go all the way.

"There are matches and there are moments. Obviously the game against South Africa is one that I'll never forget. That was a fantastic experience. It was the first time I played one of the higher tier rugby nations. I captained them that day and it was a competitive match too.

"They were the sort of memories which going back to Galway and getting that award brought back. It was a great occasion and I really appreciated it," added Farley.

Shane Sheridan, who was starting the first segment of his two-year term as president of the Clan when the presentation was made to Farley, said the Hall of Fame award is one of the many events they organise each year.

Sheridan, a solicitor in Galway, is typical of the new

HARDY PEOPLE...Connacht supporters brave the cold in Krasnoyarsk, where temperatures dropped to minus 25 degrees Celsius

Connacht Clan president Shane Sheridan

Former Connacht captain Andrew Farley is inducted into the Clan Hall of Fame in 2015

breed of Connacht supporter. He never played rugby, was not involved with any club and only took an interest in going to matches when he started studying at NUI Galway.

His father Brian is the harbour master at Galway docks, a position his father Frank held before that, real old Galway stock. Sheridan's mother Didi is from Westport where her brother Dermot Ruddy is heavily involved in Westport RFC. In turn, Ruddy's daughter Laura is an accomplished player with Galwegians RFC and the Irish sevens. The circle continues.

Connacht knew that if they were to ever grow the attendances at the Sportsground then they needed to look beyond the existing clubs and their members. They needed to introduce non-rugby people to the sport.

It was a slow process but along the way a good win over one of the Irish provinces, a big-name signing or a good run in the Challenge Cup would bring a few more and, bit by bit, attendances grew, with a surge coming in recent years when there was a proper marketing budget at their disposal.

City native Shane Sheridan knew very little about rugby when he started going to the Sportsground with a mate for a bit of craic.

"I suppose I would have started going to Connacht games when I was about 20, the archetypical casual supporter. I would have gone to two or three games that season. That would have ramped up the following year, I might have gone to five or six. I think it was 2006 that I was a season ticket holder for the first time. I ducked it for a year or two because I was studying up in Dublin. There's no point in having a season ticket when you're not going to get down to matches.

"I didn't really know the game very well when I started going. It started off as an excuse to go up and have a bit of craic. I probably was the kind of fan that I hate now! But it grew from there. Once I got into supporting it I've been an unbroken season ticket holder since 2008. A buddy of mine, we'd meet up and have a pint and go to the match but we never really interacted. I would have known nobody in the rugby circles and he wouldn't have known anyone in the rugby circles either. So we used to go and watch the match, have a drink and cheer. We would have chatted with the guys in front of us at the match and we went home."

That changed four years ago when Sheridan went to the AGM of The Clan to lend a hand, and he hasn't looked back since.

"It would have been the second season of the Clan. I happened to be in town. I remembered that the AGM was on and I went down to throw my head in to see if I could do something. It was on in the Cawley Room at the Sportsground and there were about 15 or 20 people at it. Eventually I got on the committee and since then I've made some absolutely fantastic mates."

He said that a lot of the members of the Clan are similar to him and do not come from a rugby background. Membership rose to 300 and then jumped to 400 after the Pro12 title win.

"You don't have to have played, and that's part of what we're trying to do with the Clan. You're obviously going to have that core of people that grew up playing club rugby, that come from rugby households. For them it's a no-brainer. They're always going to go to Connacht matches, they're always going to go to international matches. I suppose we're trying to cater for lads whose fathers didn't play rugby or watch rugby, but that got into rugby through watching internationals on television and coming down to the provincial games and who have fallen in love. We're trying to build a community of people who come to the Sportsground week in, week out."

The Clan was set up in 2011 with the assistance of Connacht rugby, but they are an independent group.

"We're a totally separate entity but we get great support from Connacht," added Sheridan.

"The lines of communication are always open. Sometimes people are saying things they shouldn't be saying on the forum. I know earlier on this season pictures of the new jersey leaked out and Connacht asked would we mind taking them down because we don't want to impact on the marketing plan. That's really, really important. There's great back and forth but I suppose Connacht are looking after themselves, rightly so, they're convincing people to come to games.

"In the very first year of the Clan, anybody who was a season ticket holder was a member, which made sense in the first year because it got people in. But when you have a very large membership in a club like that, you can do very little with it. We didn't have access to email addresses or names and most importantly, we didn't have access to a few bob. We started our own membership last year, it's only a tenner up front to be a member and for that you get a badge, a pin, a patch and you get a membership card to our pub sponsor Murty Rabbitt's that gives you 20 per cent off all food in there."

Busker Brownes in Cross Street was the original base for the Clan and then the nearby Dáil Bar became the headquarters for the next few years. That was before they moved to Murty Rabbitt's on Forster Street for the start of the 2016-17 season as it was nearer to the Sportsground.

THUMBS UP...An Taoiseach, Enda Kenny, enjoying the clash against Glasgow in May

The Clan really kicked off when Connacht featured in the Heineken Cup for the first time in 2011-12.

"There were many times where I was sitting in Galway and a Leinster match would be shown ahead of a Connacht match," said Sheridan. "But I remember the top floor of Buskers' that first year of the Heineken Cup was jam-packed with Connacht supporters. It was the first time outside of the Sportsground that I realised there was a real gang of people that had real interest and that would love to come along to Connacht events that aren't matches.

"There's ten people on the committee now, which is our constitutional limit. We meet once a month but we are in pretty much constant communication on the Connacht Clan forum. We have a private committee section there and it is very active.

"We have fellas from Mayo and a lady from Mayo on the committee, another fella from Connacht who lives in Clare. We have one fella who comes down from Sligo. We have another fella from Connemara but he lives in Dublin. He tries to come down as often as he can. I live in Gort. Another three live in the city or close enough to it so there's a good spread, a mix of men and women."

On match days the Clan have a section of the Clan bar which they have decorated with memorabilia over the past few years and a player is interviewed there after each game.

The Clan have built up relationships with other supporters' clubs, particularly the Irish provinces, while they also help with organising trips to away matches for fans.

They organise some charity events and donate to Connacht's chosen charities, while they have also organised a bursary for some of the academy players. The Clan is a non-profit making organisation but they also have a good range of gear and any money they raise goes back in.

"We have t-shirts, polos, pint-holders, hoodies and sweatshirts, those sort of things. It's all about getting the name out there. We try to keep the prices as low as we can. We have our own shop up on the website, that's the only place you can get them. We can't sell items in the Sportsground, which is fair enough because we don't want to clash with what Connacht are doing," added Sheridan.

The Hall of Fame awards have attracted a lot of attention. Two former players are inducted each year by the Clan, most of them from the professional era, but the likes of former Irish captain and coach Ciaran Fitzgerald has also been honoured.

It's not confined to indigenous players or other restrictions, with Clan members voting for the two recipients.

Ray Ofisa, another crowd favourite during the six years he spent at the Sportsground, was honoured before he left in 2012, a fitting reward according to Michael Bradley, the coach who brought him to Galway.

Bradley reckoned that Ofisa was one of the best players to line out for Connacht – a quiet, hard-working flanker who was capable of some massive hits.

"He's what a rugby player should be. A great work ethic, no complaining, just working hard and being as good as he can be, bringing people with him, and then being that extra bit as well. There is an X-factor there as well, two steps away from being manic, but in a very good way," said Bradley.

He recalls a match at the Sportsground where Ofisa, who rarely said a word, cut loose in the dressing room at the interval. Everyone was shocked as Ofisa was one who let his actions do the talking and rarely opened his mouth.

"Ray never really talked in meetings but he spoke at half-time once. I can't remember who we were playing but it wasn't going well and next minute Ray stood up in the dressing room and had a go. I think everyone was stunned but we all remembered one line: 'lads, nobody shits in our home, nobody shits in your home.' No one else spoke. There was no need as Ray speaking was enough, but I know we went out and won the match."

Michael Swift, another huge favourite with the fans and a player whose 15-year stint with Connacht ended just a year before they won the Pro12 title, was another recipient and the award meant a lot to him.

He was presented with the award following Connacht's 35-14 win over Munster at the Sportsground in April 2016, the first time they had done the double over an Irish province in the same season. It was also the win that guaranteed Champions Cup rugby for 2016-17, so it was a fairly raucous night.

"That was fantastic. It was great, God it was jam-packed in the Clan Bar that night.

"I gave a bit of a speech but that was after I'd enjoyed the game and enjoyed the afters, so I'm not sure how coherent my words were! But I wasn't lost for words anyway! I think neither was anyone else so they didn't really care.

"That was fantastic, to think of the support, where it's come from and where it's now. It's just sensational and to get that award was just fantastic. It's something I really appreciate," said Swift.

CHAPTER NINETEEN
_April 2016

DIARY

Connacht were the only team bidding for Pro12 glory to be still involved in European action in April and that placed extra demands on Pat Lam's squad.

Victory over Grenoble at the Stade des Alpes in the quarter-final of the Challenge Cup would ensure a schedule of four matches this month, and the general belief was that the best chance of capturing silverware for the first time lay in Europe rather than the Pro12.

That match in France would see Shane O'Leary return to his former side, Grenoble, where his former Young Munster colleague, Mike Prendergast, backs' coach with the Alpine club, had enticed him to come over for a season.

Connacht signed him from Grenoble and O'Leary knew that whatever about winning a trophy, the main priority was the top six finish.

"It would be great to win silverware this year. Any team you play on, you want to think you are about to win silverware. But we have said all year, top six, and we keep our next game focus all the time. We will keep that mindset until the end of the season," he said.

First up was a trip to Ulster but their hopes of an historic win there never materialised and they looked set for a big defeat when they trailed 18-3 in the second-half.

Connacht rallied and Caolin Blade finished off one of their tries of the season but they couldn't snatch a bonus point and finished the game with 13 men after O'Leary and Sean O'Brien were binned.

The defeat knocked Connacht to second in the table, where they remained for the rest of the campaign.

"Obviously we are very disappointed but when we were 18-3 the boys scored a great team try. It got us back in the game and when we were down to 13 men I thought the character in this team was evident in the way we held them out.

"We just didn't execute as well as we did in the past," added Lam. "Their season was on the line and they came out pretty fired-up but I was just impressed with the character the boys showed.

"With all the work we have done throughout the

season we are still in with a chance of a semi-final in the Pro12.

"And now if we perform well next week in France, a home European semi could be waiting for us. It's all about the performance."

Connacht were hoping to reach their fourth European Challenge Cup semi-final when they headed for Grenoble for what was their ninth quarter-final in the competition.

It was a cracking contest, with two tries from Niyi Adeolokun and one from Robbie Henshaw pushing Connacht 19-3 in front at one stage in the opening half, Bernard Jackman's men clawed it back to three points by the break.

A fourth try, this time from the excellent Matt Healy, looked to have set Connacht on their way to victory and a home semi-final but they were unable to close out the deal.

And while it was entirely appropriate that such a superb match would have a dramatic finish, that drama meant heartbreak for Connacht when man of the match Jonathan Wisniewski landed a drop goal to win it four minutes from time.

Grenoble had only taken the lead for the first time four minutes earlier but Connacht, despite mounting injuries, hit back immediately with a penalty from John Cooney.

Grenoble coach Jackman, who had two spells with Connacht as a player, predicted they would make a serious bid for the Pro12 crown.

"If they get a home draw, they'll be very hard to beat, but if not, I saw them against Ulster and they played very well. They can do it. To come to France and play like that is not easy. It's not easy for a young team.

"What Connacht do is look for where the space is. Even the try for Robbie Henshaw from the crossfield kick by Shane O'Leary, there's always space on a rugby field. You've just got to find it and execute, and unfortunately Connacht did execute, and we didn't.

"But in rugby there are key moments and there are different ways to win a match. We ground it out, but again, you have to say hats off to Connacht for all they put in.

"Connacht are viable candidates for a trophy. Okay,

> _'It would be great to win silverware this year. Any team you play on, you want to think you are about to win silverware.'_

HANDS OFF...Ultan
Dillane gets past
Munster's Simon Zebo

GOTCHA...Matt Healy nabs Ulster's Craig Gilroy at the Kingspan Stadium

the Challenge Cup is gone for them this year but no-one will want to play against them in the knock-out stages. I wouldn't like to play against them anyway," added Jackman.

Connacht could not afford to dwell on the disappointment with a key clash with Munster seven days later. Try-scorer Matt Healy said they planned to rebound from the defeat.

"We try and play an expansive game, and we try heads-up rugby. That's exactly how we played against Grenoble, we just coughed the ball up in certain areas.

"We are going to have to tighten up on that, and they are things we are going to have to work on this week.

"We spoke about it in the dressing room. We are holding our heads high, but feeling it in the belly, that will definitely drive us into next week, and the Munster game," said Healy.

Lam said he was confident they would deal with the challenge of readjusting mentally and physically to take on Munster.

"This competition is now over, we can't bring it back. We'll dissect the game, take what we can from it and look forward to Munster. We're looking forward to it in the Sportsground. We know we've got three games now to make the top four and we will get over this and get back into it.

"What gives us confidence is that when we beat them down in Thomond Park they had a full strength team, minus Conor Murray. We have now played so many games when teams are gunning after us and we have come through and we have just got to do this again.

"I think the big one is our support is just tremendous and we are feeding off each other. And it's not just the Connacht supporters.

"I had a lot of messages going to Grenoble from Leinster, Ulster and Munster supporters, it's fantastic. We spoke about it before the game that Ireland was right behind us, and that's a really good feeling.

"It's just a shame that we don't have the semi-final to come at home. I think the number one thing is I'm glad people are enjoying it, but more importantly, the boys enjoy the way we are playing," added Lam.

The arrival of Munster, who were struggling to secure a top six finish, ensured a full house of 7,786 supporters and Connacht could hardly have selected a better match to secure their 100th league win.

The 35-14 final scoreline told its own story as Champions Cup qualification was confirmed, leaving Connacht needing just a point from their remaining games away to Treviso and at home to champions

SO CLOSE...Matt Healy scores Connacht's fourth try against Grenoble, but there was no celebrations after this Challenge Cup quarter-final

PAIN...Andrew Browne and John Muldoon gutted after the loss in Grenoble

Glasgow Warriors in the final round.

Tries from Simon Zebo and Mike Sherry illustrated that Munster had fire in their bellies too, but Connacht's growing maturity ensured they never panicked and continued to play their running game.

They were ahead by the interval, with Niyi Adeolokun getting in for a try before their superior pack secured a penalty try. Shane O'Leary, born in Cork, reared in Limerick and Tipperary, and introduced to rugby in east Clare, turned the screw on his native province with ten points off the tee in the opening half to give his side a 20-10 lead, before adding another five after the restart.

Adeolokun made it a pair of tries for the second week in a row and new Irish international Finlay Bealham crossed for his first Connacht try in 53 appearances, although he was keen to downplay it when asked to describe the big moment.

"That is my first 'meat pie' for Connacht but the thing is after Ultan Dillane storming around there it was more of a team try. All I had to do was fall over," was how the Australian-born prop summed it up.

It was a day of milestones for Connacht, completing their first ever double over an Irish province in the league, and second only to the 34-6 win over Leinster in 2012-13 as their biggest win against one of their domestic rivals.

Lam felt it was just reward for the effort and the way players trusted their own system.

"In the last seven weeks we have had all guns blazing at us every week. That has highlighted to our players that if we prepare well and we channel everything into our game, and what we can bring, then it is going to give us our best chance.

"Whether you are expected to win or not, our own expectation is we do our jobs, perform well and that will get us through," said Lam.

The focus now switched to securing a home semi-final – the away team had never won since the knockout system was introduced in 2010 – but Lam knew they still faced a tricky tie away to Treviso.

It was Treviso's final home match and, with a final round tie away to Leinster, they needed to win to have any chance of climbing above Zebre to claim the Italian spot in the Champions Cup.

A knock to one of his knees ensured Bundee Aki wasn't risked for the trip to northern Italy where Connacht needed a point to be guaranteed a semi-final spot, but where victory was required to give them the advantage over Glasgow Warriors in the last round to secure the coveted home semi-final.

KEEP WITH US...Connacht captain John Muldoon thanks the huge band of supporters who travelled to Grenoble

APRIL 2016

UNSTOPPABLE...Niyi Adeolokun scores Connacht's third try against Munster much to the joy of Kieran Marmion and Eoin McKeon

CHAPTER TWENTY
Pat Lam

If Pat Lam achieves everything he wants to at Connacht, then he won't be missed when he leaves.

In a way it's incredible that a man who sought involvement in the most minute detail wants to install a system that will function perfectly without him, or any other individual for that matter.

Yet that is what is at the centre of his 'system', on and off the field. He strives to develop a way of doing things which is not dependent on any particular individual.

I estimate that in the three and a half years since he arrived in Galway, between midweek press conferences, pre-match and post-match interviews and other media gigs, I have interviewed him somewhere in the region of 250 times.

I can't recall one of those interviews where he didn't mention at least one of 'process', 'learnings', 'work-ons' or 'system'. Sometimes you'd get all four in the same sentence!

And he became aware of it himself: 'I know you are probably tired of me saying it, but ....,' and off he'd go again. But if we were hearing that mantra a couple of times a week, how many times was it being drilled into the players?

His method is actually very simple. You develop a style of play, you practice that at an intensity in training which is the same as in a competitive game, and you just keep repeating the process over and over until it becomes second nature, and there is no difference between the tempo you are operating at, in training or a match.

"You get to the stage in a match where you pop a pass out without looking and you know Finlay Bealham, or whoever, is there, where they should be," said Aly Muldowney. "And you do it in training and, almost miraculously, he's there again. Equally, if you are meant to be somewhere in a move, then you are there at that exact moment whether it's in training or a game. You just keep repeating over and over."

Lam, like Warren Gatland almost a quarter of a century earlier when he arrived in Galwegians to find just one ball at training, puts a huge emphasis on players practicing over and over with a ball.

He insisted, shortly after arriving at the Sportsground, that all players get a ball and have it with them at all times, even bringing it to meetings.

"That wasn't a PR stunt," said Michael Swift. "Everyone had to walk around with a ball and write on it. Pat is into his thinking outside the box, and just trying to find those one per cents. I wrote a quote from Star Wars and Yoda, it was: 'Do or do not. There is no try.' That's from Empire Strikes Back, but it has a rugby smart to it too.

"I thought he was a brave man to come out with it publicly to the players. Basically, Pat said that as a group of players, we are not good enough to win the league, or anything else, playing a normal way. We didn't have a Sonny Bill Williams who can do something out of nothing. The collective is greater than the individual and he had a huge point. It was all about the system and the process."

Lam insisted from the outset that for Connacht to be really successful, he needed to implement a style that was not dependent on a particular coach or players.

Coaches and players moved around all the time in professional sport, so he wanted to build something much more tangible.

"I've always said that at Connacht what we're trying to build with our plan is that it's not about the individual, it's about the system.

"It's professional rugby, nobody is going to stay put forever, but it can't be about just the individual or the coaching staff. People will move and you've got to set it up so that it's sustainable going through."

Joe Healy, who saw Warren Gatland embark on his coaching career at Galwegians and has closely followed his path to the top, has been hugely impressed by what has Lam has achieved.

"I am fascinated by all that I see. For me he hasn't put a foot wrong. He has actually written the script for success for a province like Connacht. I mean that in the sense that his involvement in the community, his acknowledgement of the importance of community support and what it means to Connacht, it's something that people from a different era can identify with.

"There may be people who may have a difficulty with how the game has gone in a professional context. It has just gotten away from a lot of people. Pat Lam vocalised that and he acknowledged that.

Wrapped up in Siberia

"It is very important to someone like me. It would be very easy to just say, let's recognise it for what it is, people's jobs and a profession. It would be easy to take out a cheque book and buy in 15 players to impose them on the situation and drive on and get success. I'm not sure that's sustainable.

"That's something Pat Lam has recognised in all of the success and all he has done. He won't get that without the community so that when he's gone, that's all that is left. I have an immense amount of respect for what he's doing there," said Healy.

The system that Lam implemented mapped out what each player needed to do from the moment one game finished right up to the start of the next game the following weekend.

"The final whistle goes on a Saturday, and you are almost immediately switching to the next game," said Swift. "You are getting your fluids in, compression pads on. Most of the guys invested in Sportscode, so everyone's downloading the games and analyzing them. On Monday the afternoon session might be a review and if you haven't watched it you would get found out. There were no prisoners taken, guys are expected to have prepared for it.

"You had a weekly review sheet where you set your

goals for the week, and players would usually do that on Sunday. You'd have a review of your last game, you point out three good things and three bad things, how you think your week's prep went and then looking forward to the game, and pointing out things you want to go through with your coaches. That was every week. And that alone would take about 90 minutes to properly put together. You had a physical sheet. You'd write it out and book an appointment to see Dan or Pat and go through it with them.

"It was pretty much from 8am to 4pm every day at the Sportsground, between training and meetings. Over the years, the time you spend at a rugby club increases. In my last year we had a day off on a Wednesday. A few years ago you wouldn't see anyone around the club unless he had a massage or a physio appointment. But in recent times, if you weren't at the club on a Wednesday or at least spend some time there, you were frowned upon," added Swift.

Connacht also introduced the Kitman Labs app in the past couple of years, which helped monitor the physical condition of players and flag any changes which might be occurring.

"You had to sign in every day. The first thing in the morning you answer six or seven questions, things such quality of sleep, how tired you are, your energy levels, soreness, that kind of stuff. You were rated out of ten, if your score was particularly low or below the normal number you would be flagged, the physio and Pat would get a notification.

"That would be about 6.30am on the Monday morning. The senior players would tell the younger guys, they don't want to be shown as being weak. But if you got to the club and felt tired they would know about it.

"Another question; has anything in your life had an effect on you during the weekend, your emotional levels? This would be done on an app. You would arrive every day and the first thing you had to do was go to the gym and do a series of tests. It would measure your reads, your flexibility, it was all kinds of data that they gathered. Plus you would have to go into the toilet and produce a urine sample every day. If you reached a certain level of dehydration you were not allowed to train, that was every morning," added Swift.

Mondays have always been busy at the Sportsground during the season and that intensified under the Lam regime.

A general meeting would be conducted, which would include the coaches, the medical team, marketing, media and various player groups, setting the agenda for the week. Players were in charge of different groups.

"Eoin McKeon was the IRUPA rep and he would have to say if there was something coming up. I was in charge of sponsorship and let the group know if there was any activity," added Swift. "The Monday meeting was always productive and mapped out those things for the week and subsequent weeks.

"There would be a full-squad session and it was every Monday. It would last about half-an-hour and then you go into the review session. It was fairly hot in the review sessions, but looking back we needed to be more harsh on ourselves," added Swift.

Tuesdays would generally be double sessions, with backs and forwards splitting for sessions, while one-on-one sessions would also take place.

All training sessions are recorded from a variety of angles and positions, including the use of an elevated camera, and players are able to review them directly afterwards. There are no hiding places.

"On Tuesday we'd come in and do weights and have a meeting about our attack or defence, depending on which one we didn't go through the previous day," said Aly Muldowney.

"We'd have another forwards' meeting on what we're going to do for the week. Then we go out and have our forwards' unit for half an hour or 40 minutes. We'd come

in and have a break and another meeting. Then there'd be a training session and we'd do our defence and a bit of contact. We never did too much contact, just enough, a good balance. That'd be Tuesday done, that was our big day. That was always a tough one.

"Wednesday was the day off. Some boys would come in but for me it was family day. Then Thursday, we'd come in and we'd have a meeting. We'd go through our attack, what we're going to do this week, go through all the moves. We'd have a clarity session, we'd go downstairs and walk through the attack plays," said Muldowney.

His role in the squad changed when Craig Clarke, who had been made captain after arriving from New Zealand, was forced to retire at the end of the first of a three-year deal. This was after he suffered a tenth concussion, in 22 months.

The premature end to Clarke's career was followed by the rather ignominious end to Mils Muliaina's season at the Sportsground when he was arrested live on Sky Sports in 2015, after a match in Gloucester, for a nightclub incident for which he was later acquitted.

But Muldowney said that both players had made a big impact at the Sportsground.

"I was just a front-jumping lock. I wasn't calling

Getting animated

PAT LAM

lineouts but when Craig left I had to learn to call the lineout. That was difficult at first but once I got my head around it, it was fine. Dan McFarland was great, teaching me how to call. It was tough on Craig. He was a good guy around the club, a good guy on and off the field but again, he didn't get the chance to play a lot.

"For Mils, it didn't happen as much on the field, but again, he was really good off the field about setting standards towards what the coaches should be doing. He was quite happy to stand up for the players and say if something wasn't good enough and it's good to have that," said Muldowney.

Initially, Connacht used to hold their team meetings in the Cawley Room in the branch headquarters but that space was insufficient for holding a big squad.

So they turned a big area upstairs in the gym into a meeting room, and also developed an analysis area with several computers where players can do their homework. Players were expected to be fully versed on the game plan and Swift said that players who were not up to speed faced a fairly public execution.

"There was no hiding place in the Thursday session. Traditionally that would have been a low intensity session, after all we're talking two days before a game, but that was ramped up significantly when Pat took over. You'd be tackling there as well sometimes.

"The night before the captain's run you'd be given a sheet of the game and the maps that were going to be used. They'd be all on one A4 sheet, the moves we'd be doing. But it wouldn't be uncommon to ask a few guys to stand up and challenge them on questions. If they didn't know the answers then they would be in severe trouble. Sometimes they'd even be dropped, if you didn't know your answers," added Swift.

Fionn Carr said that Lam works on attention to the small details of everything and expects everyone else to do the same.

"He gets stuck in to every facet of rugby. In fairness, as a head coach he's all across the board and he gets involved in every aspect, which is probably needed as well. He wants to know what's going on in every different area, which is probably the best thing for him. He's good in that regard. He is so thorough with everything, video analysis, detail on everything, detail on your job and game knowledge. Big detail in training, that's very important to him. He's not unlike Joe Schmidt in that regard."

Lam places demands on the people who are working around him but he leads by example and is clearly a 24/7 operator.

On away match days all members of management are expected to present themselves for a 5km morning jog. It gets them in the zone and has become a ritual.

Long before Lam was successful with Connacht he was going out into the community, willing to talk and share experiences. He is not the first Connacht coach to do that, it was happening back at the start of the professional era and before that.

But Lam has continued to do it after Connacht's historic triumph. At a fundraising event for one of his children's school, he volunteered to get the ball rolling by contributing the fee he was promised for attending a corporate management speaking event he was doing in Dublin the following week.

In October, Lam brought the Connacht squad to Kinvara in south Co Galway to open and train on the new sports pitch developed by Seamount College.

There's no rugby in the school or the seaside village but the principal Maighréad Mhic Dhomhnaill noted the shared history with Connacht and wrote to Lam asking him to open what she described as their 'Sportsground'.

Ten years earlier the school was listed for closure but fought a successful battle and now has over 400 students and 30 staff. One of the key people involved in 2006 in the battle to save the school was Iain O'Brien. He died in 2012 from cancer, aged in his late 40s. His son Sean won a Pro12 medal when he came on at half-time in Murrayfield against Leinster.

That wasn't the reason Lam brought the Connacht squad there to open their new facility. Lam, himself a former schoolteacher, could appreciate the battle the school had gone through to keep its doors open.

He spoke movingly to the children about how they should deal with issues in life, he told them about being bullied himself in school, and the need for them to talk about their problems and how to address their fears. A week before Connacht went there, the father of one of the students committed suicide. Another person in the village did likewise shortly before that.

Lam encouraged the children to talk about their feelings. Jake Heenan, the former New Zealand U-20 captain, and an IRUPA 'Tackle Your Feelings' ambassador, also spoke to the teenagers, as did John Muldoon.

Lam may ultimately achieve his aim of leaving Connacht with a system in place that is not dependent on the individual.

But there are many places in Connacht where they will never forget Pat Lam and, in a lot of cases, it will have nothing to do with rugby.

That will probably be his best achievement in the west of Ireland.

Pat Lam with his Pro12 coach of the season award, and (below) he embraces his captain John Muldoon after their historic win over Leinster in the final

CHAPTER TWENTY ONE
Success

Perhaps one of the lowest points in Connacht's history in the professional era came off the field rather than on it. The 2007-08 Magners League campaign was launched at a glitzy ceremony in the Liberty Stadium in Swansea, which had been opened two years earlier.

Connacht team manager Tim Allnutt and captain Andrew Farley, who had played for Swansea, were among those who attended that launch in August 2007, along with representatives from the nine other clubs.

One of the main parts of the launch was a segment on a big screen showing highlights from the previous season. They dimmed the lights, cranked up the music and for the next few minutes the audience was treated to a host of tries, big hits, fist-pumping and other celebrations from all the teams in the league. Well, all the teams bar Connacht!

"They just forgot about us, mate," said Allnutt. "It was almost as if we didn't exist. They kept showing teams over and over but there wasn't a glimpse of Connacht."

Connacht weren't long in throwing in a few broadsides, with red-faced officials apologising for the blunder. But perhaps the most telling indictment of where Connacht stood in the pecking order came with the explanation from the league's organisers.

"All of the footage used in the DVD compilation for the launch of the 2007-08 Magners League season was provided to us by our TV partners. Unfortunately, there was no TV coverage of any of Connacht's 2006/2007 season home games," a Magners League spokesperson said.

The reality at the time was that Connacht usually only featured on television when they were playing away to one of the bigger sides. Their omission from the promotion at the launch of the 2007-08 season was made all the more difficult to accept when Allnutt and Farley noted that Border Reivers, who had been disbanded at the end of the previous season, featured prominently in the DVD.

A DVD of a different nature was viewed by Pat Lam when he was looking at moving from New Zealand to take charge of Connacht.

'The West's Awake', a superb fly-on-the-wall documentary, was released in 2012. Produced by Kieran Hartigan, it charted Connacht's first season participating in the Heineken Cup and went behind the scenes as Eric Elwood and his men prepared the province to meet a new challenge.

It was a tough season but not even a 14-match losing run could shatter their spirits and the pressure-valve which was released when they finally ended the run by knocking Harlequins out of the Heineken Cup was just unreal. It made great footage and showed what Connacht could do.

"I did a lot of homework before I got here," said Lam. "I needed to know who I represented. I watched 'The West's Awake' documentary, to see all that emotion, what it meant to people here. You start to feel an affinity, to see similarities between Ireland and Western Samoa. It's about family and community, and that's why is it easy to connect here."

Connacht were always capable of producing a shock result but none was quite as stunning as the 16-14 win over Toulouse in the Heineken Cup in December 2013. It was a truly astonishing result, as the most prolific winners of the tournament, the only side to win it four times, were turned over in their own backyard. It was enough for the renowned French sports newspaper *L'Équipe* to put the outcome on their front page the following morning.

"We have a team with no superstars," said Lam outside the dressing room in Stade Ernest Wallon afterwards. "We missed so many opportunities throughout the season, but we still came here confident. We just had to make sure that everyone did their job.

"We had a lot of belief coming to this game. Although we are at the bottom of the table this year, every single game we played, we could have won."

Connacht and their supporters celebrated that Sunday evening in one of the toughest grounds in France as if they had won the trophy.

But for a long time it appeared it would just be remembered as one of those freakish results. Connacht went into the game having lost four contests on the spin and they were defeated in five of their next seven games, starting with a 37-9 loss to Toulouse at the Sportsground, six days after the triumph in France.

"When I got here I spent 50 hours, an hour with each player, and I still do it with every player that works with

KING'S CHAIR...
Darragh Leader and Niyi Adeolokun carry Matt Healy from the field after victory in La Rochelle in January 2015

JOY...Dan Parks and Craig Ronaldson celebrate Connacht's famous Heineken Cup win in Toulouse in 2013

OLD HANDS...Ronan Loughney and Michael Swift enjoy victory over Bayonne in 2014, a win which Swift described as one of his most enjoyable

me," said Lam. "I ask them certain questions, such as, obviously, what their big goal is. And then I get right through to the end and it's a one-pager. The last bit of the questioning, when I understand what they're trying to do, I ask them what they want from me as a coach. At the end, I tell them: 'this is what I want from you'. So you get a very good connection there."

Connacht played 28 matches in Lam's first season, winning nine and losing 19. By the end of the second season they won 14 out of 30, losing 15 and drawing one, moving to their highest place since the league went home and away, when they finished seventh.

Gloucester beat them in the quarter-finals of the European Challenge Cup and then edged them by 40-32 in a cracking Champions Cup play-off game in May.

The integration of academy players was paying a big dividend and the foundation was laid to have a crack at success heading into the 2015-16 campaign.

"The way rugby's going, you need your squad," said Fionn Carr. "You need a full squad and the academy guys coming through were bigger, stronger and faster.

"We used to do a lot of team-on-team sessions and the lads would rotate in and out. With those types of sessions that we did under Pat, you do need everyone. It makes you a better player in a competitive environment.

"With 15-on-15 and even 10-on-10 it was good for the academy guys to step in and train at that intensity. When they were called upon, they were generally able to slot straight in. We knew after our second year with Pat that we had structures and processes in place. Everyone had an idea of the direction Pat was going. We changed a bit but we didn't change a huge amount. Lads stepped it up with regard to areas like game knowledge, detail.

"Basically we played as we trained, which is a massive thing. The fact that training was recorded it meant that if you did have a bad session, you knew straight away. People were training like they were going to play so when it came to game-time, you were able to implement what you did in training. That intensity and that competitiveness is what brought us to the next level in that third year, the year we won the cup."

The second foray into the Heineken Cup heralded the arrival of the first superstar of the professional era in Connacht, with Robbie Henshaw going from winning a Connacht schools cup title with Marist College in March 2012, to playing in Europe's top competition just over six months later.

The Athlone native came through the academy in Connacht and was capped for the first time in the

Robbie Henshaw celebrates with Dan Parks after his late drop goal against Biarritz in the Champions Cup in 2012, and (right) lifts the Connacht senior schools cup for Marist College earlier that year

SUCCESS

159

BIG STEP...Bundee Aki and Caolin Blade enjoy March's win over Leinster

summer of 2013 against the United States, just a few days short of his 20th birthday.

Henshaw signed a two-year deal a few months after making his debut in September 2012, which was later extended by a year, but the Pro12 final win over Leinster was his final game for Connacht – for now at least.

His move to Leinster, after signing a three-year contract, was a tough pill for Connacht fans to swallow, especially when they went on and won the Pro12 title after he had made the decision.

It remains to be seen if he ever comes back to Connacht but supporters will be encouraged by comments he made on the summer tour to South Africa.

"As I said to a number of Connacht fans: 'this is not goodbye; it could be see you later in the future'. Anything could happen around the corner. But to finish in the way I did with the team I've been with for four years, and when I was a kid, is incredible."

Lam's philosophy of training the way you want to play began to feed into an increase in consistency on the pitch and it was reflected in the team's results as the 2015-16 kicked off.

They won nine of their opening ten matches in the league and Europe, but it was the 18-12 win in Thomond Park in November which really suggested that they were poised for big things.

The Limerick venue had been a graveyard for Connacht down through the decades and their previous win at Thomond Park was back in the amateur days in 1986, an 11-9 win which was achieved with Davy Henshaw, Robbie's uncle, playing at tighthead.

Aly Muldowney was only in Connacht a few seasons but he knew the significance of finally beating Munster on their own patch in the professional era.

"I'd only been in Connacht for a couple of years but it was huge. That was one of the best experiences I ever had. It was unreal, the way we beat them, the way we played. Everyone was starting to come together with that system. From that game, we raised the bar on how we played our 2-4-2 system and how we can rip teams apart. We weren't as clinical, we could have finished off a few more opportunities but that was massive for us."

Connacht got turned over in Cardiff the following Friday and lost five of their next six games. It looked like their season would fizzle out before the spring.

Former Connacht hooker Jerry Flannery, the Munster scrum coach, noticed though how they regrouped and how injuries didn't greatly impact on them as the players coming in seemed to raise the bar.

"During the Pro12 games over the Six Nations I

BRIGHT SPARK...Robbie Henshaw is congratulated by Eoin Griffin and Sean Henry following his Heineken Cup try against Zebre in 2012

thought they had injuries and lads dropping out, but it was next man up. That is reflective of a really good culture and environment. That's good coaching and good management.

"It's a good environment where it's not built around individuals. That's a very strong ethos. When people started dropping like flies I knew there was an edge there with Connacht. The way they played, their game plan, it really got the best out of the players. It takes time to bed that in. Pat Lam was afforded the time and it paid off."

Grenoble ended Connacht's run in the Challenge Cup but their coach Bernard Jackman also noticed some big fundamental changes in his former side.

"The week we played Connacht, I highlighted how good they were to our guys and I showed clips to reinforce that. But I think our players probably felt that the three best Irish teams were Leinster, Munster and Ulster.

"There was a danger of underestimating Connacht. But after the game they thought: 'Wow, that's a good team and that's a team that have spirit, have quality'. We felt an attachment to Connacht, the way they handled themselves after the game. It was a bone-crushing defeat for them. They could have blamed several

incidents of mistakes, refereeing decisions, bad luck or whatever, but they didn't. I thought they were very mature, they were a team with a lot of self-belief. They were just waiting to embrace success," said Jackman.

Michael Swift had seen it all by the time he retired in 2014 but he could see the potential developing in his final years at the Sportsground.

"A couple of years before I retired we played Bayonne away. It was one of my most memorable games because the squad was so young and we went there and won. It showed how far we had come.

"In other years, when we had to send a young team, you could immediately see the difference and we would get beaten, sometimes quite heavily.

"The academy has played a huge role, those seeds were sown years ago. Near the end of my career it was more like a crèche some times in the Sportsground. We had our senior dressing room so it wasn't as bad, but in the communal area you see all of these guys using Snapchat or whatever and you think: 'what has happened here?' And then you realise, 15 years go by in a flash.

"At various times you could see the green shoots appearing. You just hoped the day would come when it would all deliver. It has now, success at last," said Swift.

BIG STATEMENT...Fionn Carr and Eoin McKeon bask in the glory of that triumph at Stade Ernest Wallon in Toulouse 2013

CHEERS!...Andrew Browne, Ethienne Reynecke, John Muldoon, Mike McCarthy, Eoin McKeon and Mata Fifita enjoy a beer after beating Glasgow in 2013

AULD ENEMY...Beating Leinster is always a sweet feeling for Connacht as Andrew Browne and Ronan Loughney celebrate in March 2016

SUCCESS

CHAPTER TWENTY TWO
May 2016

DIARY

It's fair to say that traditionally, Connacht were not a side programmed to be competitive in the month of May. Usually by then plans were being put in place for pre-season and the hope that they could hit the ground running at the start of the next campaign.

Players were thinking of holidays, some of them moving to new clubs, others still searching for a new destination, while those staying on needed to get away from it all and regroup.

The results bore this out. In the 15 years of the league, Connacht had won their opening match a dozen times and lost just three.

But they only ever managed to win their final game three times, suffering losses 12 times in the final round of matches.

Often their season didn't extend into May but when it did, they lost 18 of the 21 matches played in that month.

Eight of the 12 teams in the league would be finished their season before 5pm on 7 May 2016 but Connacht, and their final round opponents Glasgow Warriors, were assured of a semi-final spot. They were playing for home advantage, knowing that all previous 12 semi-finals were won by the hosts. That didn't change in 2016.

Connacht decided to approach the showdown with Glasgow the same as any other game, by trusting the 2-4-2 game-plan which had served them so well.

"Pat brought in that game-plan a couple of seasons ago," said Tiernan O'Halloran. "The confidence grew from there, we trust the system and each other.

"With the weather getting the way it is, dry ball and good pitches will suit us more and more. We are really looking forward to it now, coming into the business end of the season," he said.

Another full house of 7,786 packed into the Sportsground for the fixture. Glasgow were one of just two teams in the league that Connacht had failed to defeat since Pat Lam arrived three years earlier – Ulster were the other – but they changed that in no uncertain manner, with a deserved 14-7 win.

Bundee Aki, finishing the campaign with awesome power, got in for the opening try after 18 minutes thanks to good work from AJ MacGinty and Kieran Marmion. MacGinty converted and the Sportsground was rocking.

Connacht took that 7-0 lead into the break but the champions hit back through a converted try from Scottish loosehead Gordon Reid.

Then Tongan tighthead Sila Puafisi was shown a straight red card when he led with his head into a ruck, and the champions played out the remaining half hour with 14 men.

The winning score came shortly afterwards when a crossfield kick from replacement Shane O'Leary picked out Tiernan O'Halloran and the Clifden full-back crowned his 100th appearance for Connacht with the try which secured them a home semi-final against the same opposition two weeks later.

The home semi-final ensured that the 'sold out' signs were up for the fourth game in a row and as a conversation developed in the west about the need to develop a bigger stadium.

"It's massive for us, it's massive for our fans," said Lam.

"I think everyone was expecting the result would go the other way. Not only that we beat them, the way we beat them is what I'm proud about. They are a phenomenal team, they're going to come back stronger."

Glasgow coach Gregor Townsend, whose side came to Galway on the back of a nine-match winning run, felt they could become the first side to win an away semi-final, not least as the red card for Puafisi had a bearing.

"We played a team last year in a similar circumstance, Ulster, last game of the season. We won and then they came back the following week and played really well against us," said Townsend.

"We'd prefer to be at home and we were all out to try and win this game and play at home but we know the opposition much better than we did going into today."

The home semi-final ensured that the 'sold out' signs were up for the fourth game in a row and as a conversation developed in the west about the need to develop a bigger stadium, Lam wanted his players to stay grounded. He did not want them to settle for just a semi-final, not when they were this close.

WELL DONE...Bundee Aki is congratulated by Niyi Adeolokunafter he gets the vital touch against Glasgow Warriors

'YOU PUT YOUR LEFT LEG IN'...Bundee Aki leads the dancing after Connacht clinch a home semi-final by beating Glasgow Warriors

"It's massive for us and it's massive for our fans to get a home semi-final. The boys were so excited because now we can show people what we can do.

"A lot's been talked about the game and our skill level. I said to the boys, it was about showing people our desire, our character, our culture. That was the one ingredient missing last week against Treviso.

"We played some good rugby against them but they wanted it more. We put a big focus on that, the boys came back and delivered it in spades. I'm so proud of them. It was a great effort," added Lam.

Connacht again prepared for the semi-final the same as they did for any other game and winger Matt Healy said that players were very comfortable with that approach.

"In terms of our approach to games, it is always the same and Pat's been driving that since he's come in, since day one.

"So in that sense we are very much going out in the semi-final to play our game. Obviously, after that Grenoble defeat, it kind of hit home to us that coming into the last few games of the season, we need to tighten up on our defensive game and stuff like that.

"There was a little touch up that we addressed in terms of closing games out. But our approach has always been the same going into any match so I think you can expect more of that next time," said Healy.

It was only the third time in the history of the competition that Connacht had played the same team in successive matches, and they were bidding to defeat the same team in succession for the first time in the league. In March 2011 they defeated Aironi 11-6 at the Sportsground and then just over two weeks later they went down 25-13 away to the Italians.

The only other time Connacht played the same opposition in successive matches in the league was earlier in the 2015-16 season when they lost 21-19 away to Scarlets on January 10 but then on January 30 they scored a 30-17 victory over the Llanelli side at the Sportsground, which turned their season around.

That was the start of a six-match winning run, three away from home, which ultimately sent Connacht through to their first Pro12 semi-final.

Captain John Muldoon warned of a backlash from Glasgow and that the holders would be going to the limit to hold on to their crown.

"They will feel they can do an awful lot better than the last day. But we would feel that way as well. The conditions didn't suit either team so it was a matter of grinding out a win," he said.

BEARD RASH...Aly Muldowney and John Muldoon after defeating the champions

THANK HEAVENS...Rodney Ah You and Bundee Aki take a moment to reflect on securing a home semi-final

GOOD LUCK...Former Connacht forwards' coach Dan McFarland of Glasgow Warriors and Connacht skills coach Dave Ellis

Coach Lam urged fans to paint the region green as they prepared to reach the first ever final in the province's 131-year history.

And in a week when Connacht laid out their strategic plan for the next four years, which included the development of a 10,000 capacity stadium, Lam said this was an exciting time for rugby in the province.

"There are flags everywhere, jerseys everywhere, everyone's going green," said the Connacht coach.

"The fans know they've been part of this journey the whole way through, and we've been so pleased to get a home semi because it is a magical place here."

The demand for tickets, for the fourth game in a row, outstripped supply but Lam urged fans who couldn't get to the game to make sure they were still part of the occasion.

'If you're not at the ground, have a barbecue and just build up. Have people around and enjoy the occasion. We know what we represent."

Connacht were bidding to become the tenth side to reach the league final, with six different clubs having won the 14 finals to date.

There was a highly charged atmosphere at the Sportsground all day for the 6.30pm kick-off, with Italian referee Marius Mitrea in charge. He had also officiated

at their loss in Llanelli in January and was the only non-Irish or Welsh referee to take charge of a Connacht game during their glorious Pro12 season.

Connacht knew that the champions would aim for an early strike but Glasgow's hopes suffered a massive double blow when they lost out-half Finn Russell and tighthead Zander Fagerson after just a minute, following a horrible collision between the two Scottish internationals.

There was an early exchange of penalties from AJ MacGinty and Duncan Weir but Glasgow, who also lost flanker Adam Ashe to injury, never looked like building a lead with the wind and it was Connacht who went in with a 10-3 lead when Niyi Adeolokun struck three minutes from the break.

A grubber from the superb Bundee Aki deceived Glasgow full-back Stuart Hogg and neither Weir nor his scrum-half Henry Pyrgos managed to hold the Connacht winger as he sprinted home from 40 metres to score under the posts. MacGinty added the easy conversion.

Glasgow hit back through the brilliance of Leone Nakarawa after 49 minutes, but Connacht still led when Weir was unable to land the difficult conversion from the left.

MacGinty extended Connacht's lead to 13-8 after 53

ON OUR WAY...Niyi Adeolokun runs in Connacht's only try of the semi-final

minutes with a penalty in front of the posts after another bout of sustained pressure, but Weir cancelled that out four minutes later with a good kick from 25 metres.

Connacht got back on top and MacGinty made it 16-11 with 16 minutes left on the clock, as the crowd willed them home.

Connacht thought they had it wrapped up nine minutes from time when Adeolokun got over in the right corner after Aki had forced a superb turnover after a big hit on Weir but they were whistled back and the try was disallowed for accidental offside.

And Connacht's task got more difficult two minutes later when replacement tighthead Rodney Ah You was sin-binned for a reckless high challenge on Hogg, leaving Connacht with 14 men for the closing seven minutes.

But they never let their grip slip and the final whistle was greeted with a pitch invasion which would have done justice to an All-Ireland final.

And a GAA hero wasn't far from the thoughts of an emotional John Muldoon as he came to terms with Connacht, in his 13th season, reaching their first final in 131 years.

The previous night former GAA president and Galway hurler Joe McDonagh had died after a brief illness.

McDonagh famously sang 'The West's Awake' after Galway's 1980 breakthrough All-Ireland hurling title and Muldoon said the death fired him up as he prepared to lower the champions.

"I thought of Joe McDonagh and I would like to think that the west is awake tonight in his memory as much as it is for us.

"It is brilliant to be in a final, I can't believe it. It's unreal. We will head to Edinburgh now and try finish the job," said Muldoon.

Glasgow coach Gregor Townsend said that while they were bitterly disappointed to surrender their crown, he could have few complaints and he said the thriller at a packed Sportsground brought out the best in the Pro12.

"It's a great advert for the league, a fantastic atmosphere and I wish Connacht well in the final. Connacht have played positive rugby throughout and deserve their place," he said.

Coach Pat Lam, who revealed that Aki had been a doubt before the game with an injury picked up midweek in training, said these were special days to be with Connacht.

"What a game. The lads showed people what the fans and the whole province means to us. I knew that would bring it out and bring our game on another level.

"I'm so pleased for the people, not just here but back home as well, Sligo, Leitrim, Roscommon, Mayo and Galway. It's fantastic, phenomenal. The Sportsground with no-one here, it's pretty average but as soon as the people come in, it's magical.

"What we have to acknowledge is the only reason we play well at the Sportsground is the supporters, that's what gets us through. It's a magical place. They lift us, we lift them, it's just great. It's not the Sportsground, it's the people. It's like any place, it's not the west of Ireland, it's the people of the west of Ireland that make the difference and that's what we've always talked about; it's people not places," said Lam.

He said that the final was a golden opportunity for such a young side to lay down a marker as individuals and as a team.

"It's a great education for these boys. For a lot of them it's their first final, the guys are learning. The average age of the team is only 25 once you take Muldoon and Muldowney out of it. It's exciting for Connacht. There's a lot of good players coming through and it's great to be able to represent the west," added Lam.

The pre-match fever for a final, for so long only associated with the hurling and football teams heading to All-Ireland finals, now switched to rugby.

Getting tickets for the final in Murrayfield, unlike Croke Park on All-Ireland final day, was not a problem but the difficulty lay in getting accommodation in Edinburgh. The city's marathon was also scheduled for that weekend and there was hardly a hotel room left in the Scottish capital.

Even the squad, who decided to go over a day early, had to switch hotels as they could not get accommodation in the Marriott Hotel which the Pro12 organisers had reserved for them for the night before the match. So they stayed at the Village Hotel on the Thursday before the final.

There was little time for fans to make arrangements to travel, with Leinster supporters having had an extra day to book after their semi-final win over Ulster.

In the end, some fans stayed in Glasgow, others in Newcastle, more at various towns around Scotland. Ferries from Dublin and Belfast were booked up, flights were either taken direct to Scotland or else to England, with the rest of the journey completed by train or car.

After waiting 131 years to get to a final, getting to Scotland for the showdown was never going to be an insurmountable obstacle and in the end an estimated 10,000 made the journey for what turned out to be a record 34,550 attendance for a Pro12 final.

Tiernan O'Halloran, whose father Aidan, a former

Connacht president, had won an All-Ireland Gaelic football medal with Offaly when they killed Kerry's hopes of five titles in a row in 1982, knew that winning a trophy would be an enormous boost for the game in the west.

"It's hard to put into words what silverware would do for this province, because it's been such an incredible rise this season.

"You walk through town any day of the week and you'll see kids in Connacht in jerseys all over the place. Five years ago, you might see one every three or four weeks; it would be mainly Gaelic football or hurling jerseys.

"So, that's the way it's gone. Rugby has grown in the province as a whole, it'll hopefully encourage younger guys coming up in school and in Gaeltacht areas especially to pick up a rugby ball as well as a sliotar or a football.

"That'll just help to grow the province. The future of Connacht rugby is going to get better and better if success breeds success. If we can win the final, it can grow even more," he said.

TOP GUY...Man of the match Bundee Aki is swamped by Connacht supporters as they reach the Pro12 final

'AND SHAKE IT ALL ABOUT'...Bundee Aki leads the victory dance after the semi-final win over Glasgow Warriors

'AND HERE'S WHAT WE WILL DO'...Pat Lam plots a course for the final in Murrayfield

CHAPTER TWENTY THREE
__The Match

The journey began 15 years earlier, on an August Saturday afternoon in Cardiff, and having continued through 27 venues across Ireland, Wales, Scotland and Italy, Connacht were now in a position to bid for their first league title.

History weighed heavily upon them; this wasn't just the league crown they were looking for, but the first bit of silverware since they were founded in 1885.

And having come this far, captain John Muldoon was determined they wouldn't settle for second best.

"It's probably hard to believe, but we have been talking about winning a final for a good few weeks and months now. We probably haven't been saying that too loud. But we have been speaking about it. We reassessed our goals a good few months back and all roads were pointing at Edinburgh."

The final would be Connacht's 285th league match since they kicked off their first Celtic League campaign with a memorable 6-3 win over Cardiff at the Arms Park on 18 August 2001.

There was many a twist and turn since then but the bare facts show that Connacht won 102 of those games, drew 11 and lost 171. Almost a quarter of those wins – 25 – came in the 2014-15 and 2015-16 seasons.

That clearly illustrated the progress made under Pat Lam, who brought skills' coach Dave Ellis and backs' coach Andre Bell with him from New Zealand to the Sportsground. He supplemented that backroom team with Dan McFarland as forwards' coach and another former Connacht player, Conor McPhillips, as performance analyst.

And when McFarland left for Glasgow Warriors in the summer of 2015, Lam found another gem in ex-Connacht player and academy coach Jimmy Duffy, who took over.

'We were 100 per cent that we'd get the win. To be honest, we were more concerned, I don't know why, but we were more concerned about playing Ulster. We knew could beat Leinster because we had beaten them.'

Clearly, it was a management team which worked well and the input of each of them was clear to see as the season progressed, with Connacht building up a head of steam in the hunt for a crown that they were 50-1 outsiders to collect at the start of the season.

Those odds, of course, were negligible compared to the 5,000-1 which Leicester City found themselves at in August 2015 before they embarked on the most unlikely journey ever to win the Premier League in England. To put that in perspective, you would only get odds of 2,000-1 in August 2015 on Elvis Presley being found alive!

Unsurprisingly, comparisons were made between Connacht and Leicester City as they both headed for glory.

"We have watched Leicester, of course we have and there are similarities," said Muldoon. "Three or four years ago we were bottom of the league, so it's hard to fathom where we have come from. But again you are talking about a young team, learning all the time.

"We haven't won anything as a team together, but you have a lot of people who have won competitions – Tom McCartney with the Blues, Bundee Aki with the Chiefs – and you have a lot of young fellas there who have come through and won different competitions.

"When you are out there, you are playing cup rugby. It's been questioned at times this season, can we finish out games? Have we the knowledge and have we the wherewithal to finish out games."

The seven-day gap between the semi-final win over Glasgow Warriors and the showdown with Leinster meant that Connacht didn't have time to get distracted by the build-up to the biggest day in their history.

And lock Aly Muldowney, set to play his final match after three seasons before moving to Grenoble, said it never entered their heads all week that they might lose the final.

"We were 100 per cent that we'd get the win. To be honest, we were more concerned, I don't know why, but we were more concerned about playing Ulster. We knew we could beat Leinster because we had beaten them. They beat us too but we knew that if we played well on the day, we could beat them.

"Ulster, I think I've lost every time I've played them.

CAPTAIN'S HONOUR...John Muldoon becomes the first Connacht man in the province's 131-year history to lift a trophy

Bundee Aki and Eoin McKeon

John Muldoon is swamped

FRONT MEN...Rodney Ah You, Tom McCartney and Finlay Bealham

seconds. I don't know where the time went.

"It was unreal at the finish, it was ridiculous. We got the trophy, lots of champagne, a lap of honour. I went and got my kids, took them around. That was unreal. I went into the stand to see my dad and Sam, my wife. It was special, it really was.

"It was mayhem in the changing room. The boys who weren't playing had been drinking all day so it was pretty loose in there! I got changed and went out to see my cousins and my dad again, to say goodbye to them as they were heading home," said Muldowney.

Bernard Jackman was watching the match between two of his former teams at his home beside Stade Lesdiguieres in Grenoble. He had friends involved in both camps.

"I'm very close to Jimmy Duffy and Conor McPhillips, having played with both of them and, of course, John Muldoon. There are not many guys still left there since I left. But I just think that for Connacht to win it was phenomenal, especially the way they played.

"I thought Connacht deserved it more and I'm glad they won it. I like the way they play. I use Connacht and Leicester City as an example. For clubs like us in Grenoble who don't have the budgets of the others, Leicester City and Connacht are brilliant examples,

brilliant champions," said Jackman.

The match-day squad members were presented with their medals on the field and other players within the squad received their medals in the changing room. Connacht subsequently purchased medals for the remainder of the squad involved during the season, along with members of management, and presented them at a function during the summer.

Fionn Carr received his medal in the changing room, a fitting way to end his six seasons with Connacht over two terms, departing as the province's all-time top try scorer.

"I realised fairly early on we were going to win it. The lads played really well and Leinster didn't seem to have an answer on the day. We had all our structures in place. The game plan was there and the guys who played executed it fairly well. Once the game got on and the lads started throwing the ball around and playing the game we had been playing all year you just had that feeling that they were going to kick on and win which they did."

Gerry Kelly, the chief executive who carried Connacht from 1999 to when he retired in 2012, travelled on a day charter, forking out €500 for the trip. The Pro12 tournament director David Jordan, an old friend, had

TRY ME!...Tiernan O'Halloran, Matt Healy and Niyi Adeolokun, who scored Connacht's three tries in the final

offered to get him hospitality tickets, but Kelly decided to watch the match with another former Connacht president, Joe Daly, and Daly's son Martin, who are from Creggs.

After the game, he headed across to the other stand and bumped into Leinster chief executive Mick Dawson outside the hospitality area. Dawson, realising that Kelly didn't have a ticket, took off his own accreditation and put it around Kelly's neck. "You need to be in there today, of all days, much more than I do," said Dawson.

"One of the first guys I saw when I went in was the union president Martin O'Sullivan, and the first words I said to him were 'thank you'. Martin had been a huge supporter of Connacht in the last few years and played a key role in getting us on the road. I was delighted to meet him and thank him and it crowned such a glorious day," said Kelly.

Connacht fans were rejoicing throughout the world and so too were former players.

Andrew Farley was on a business trip to the United States. It was breakfast time in San Francisco and he was trying to get a stream of the game on his laptop.

"I missed the start, I couldn't get a stream. A couple of the Connacht Clan messaged me on Twitter asking if I was going to watch it and I said I was.

"I was in my hotel room but the stream just kept stuttering. I reckon I missed probably the first 30 minutes and then I thought radio and I started listening to the radio. Then Lucy, my wife, was texting me. She was in France but obviously it was on Sky so she was texting me going: 'They're going so well.' During the second-half it was cutting in and out and I was getting frustrated but as soon as I heard that final whistle, I was delighted.

"I was so happy for the guys who I knew that were involved, and for the club, and obviously for the city and county of Galway and the region of Connacht and everyone that's ever worn the jersey. It was a proud moment."

Pat Lam, who had reminded people a few times in recent weeks that he had been fired from his previous coaching job at Auckland Blues in 2012, was thrilled with the victory but was already throwing down the gauntlet for further success.

"We're back on June 30th. I've already set the goals for next year. We've got to go and defend this and go back-to-back in the Pro12.

"It's realistic for us to try and win it again. The second one then is, I want to try and get into the knockout stages of the Champions Cup. That's the key, you set goals and you work every day to meet them."

John Muldoon had set many goals over the previous 13 seasons but there was never a moment like this; a man-of-the-match performance from the 34-year old on the day when he became the first man to lift a rugby trophy for Connacht.

"My heart rate is still up there, it's absolutely phenomenal," said Muldoon afterwards. "You dream of days like this and you dream of being part of days like this. It definitely hasn't sunk in yet, it's absolute euphoria in there.

"I'm delighted for the lads. We spoke all week about wanting to go out there and perform and do what we did all year. And I think we did that. That's the most pleasing aspect of it, the fact that we didn't go into our shells. It's just phenomenal.

"I'm delighted for everybody inside. I got emotional a couple of times. I thought I was done and then Eric came in, and that set me off again then. I've said it for the last few weeks, there's a lot of people who have put more into it than I have, and a lot of people are supporting Connacht rugby longer than me, and they'll be proud tonight and they'll enjoy this as much as we will."

George Naoupu and John Muldoon

Bundee Aki and Kieran Marmion

Skills coach Dave Ellis, backs' coach Andre Bell, Pat Lam, team manager Tim Allnutt, CEO Willie Ruane, forwards' coach Jimmy Duffy and head performance analyst Conor McPhillips with the Pro12 trophy

HEALING HANDS...Connacht's physio David Hanly, Dr John O'Donnell, masseur Robbie Fox, head physio Garrett Coughlan and Dr Donal 'Ginger' O'Beirne get the reward for their hard work

FAMILY TIES...John Muldoon's mother Claire and his aunt Una congratulate him after he captained Connacht to win the Pro12 title

THE AKI FILES...Bundee grabs a selfie

CHAPTER TWENTY FOUR
The Homecoming

Spare a thought for Michael Swift, Connacht's longest-serving player in the professional era.

Swift played 264 league and European games for Connacht over a 15-year period but finally listened to his body's aches and hung up his boots at 37 years of age in the summer of 2015.

He probably holds a record for the most one-year contract extensions signed by a professional rugby player, but no sooner had he retired than Connacht went and won their first silverware in history, inside 12 months.

And then, at the other end of the spectrum, is Cormac Brennan – a 21-year-old utility back who finished the 2015-16 season as a Pro12 winner, despite not having played a single minute of competitive rugby for Connacht.

The promising three-quarter from across Galway Bay in Ballyvaughan, Co Clare, was on the bench for the clash away to Ulster in April, and while he didn't get a run, that was enough to earn him a Pro12 medal.

The bright prospect joined Galwegians because it was the nearest club to him from where he lived in the Burren, and will hopefully go on to have great days with Connacht. But he may well go down in history as the only player to make his Pro12 debut with a winner's medal already in his back pocket.

But the contrasting fortunes of Swift and Brennan just sum up how sport can deal different hands.

Swift, though, wasn't feeling sorry for himself and he celebrated the final win over Leinster as if he was out on the field himself.

"You always think 'one more year' and I could have possibly been on the stage with them getting the trophy. But I had 15 wonderful years and for me it was all about retiring when I did. It was the perfect time for me.

"I'm just thrilled for everyone involved. I know what it means to people.

"I had 15 wonderful years and the last year was probably the hardest for me. That one extra year might well have been ten extra years with the way the body was feeling and stuff like that. The body just doesn't allow that," he said.

He said that it was a nice touch that Pat Lam and John Muldoon made former players and management

as much part of the victory as possible, and Swift said that Connacht players down through the years shared in the historic success.

"John Muldoon talked about the players who had worn the jersey leading up to that day and it was as much a celebration of those guys and an acknowledgement of players and management who were at the club.

"Everyone can take a small chunk of that, including the supporters as well – they are as much a part of this journey as the players," added Swift.

He was unable to get to the match in Edinburgh but he and his wife Jill jumped in the car early on Sunday morning to be part of the homecoming celebrations in Galway.

Many other former players did the same, travelling from all over the country to join up with their former colleagues.

He bumped into former scrum-half Chris Keane shortly after arriving in Galway. Keane, too, had driven from Dublin that morning to be part of the homecoming, having spent six years with Connacht until he returned to his native Leinster in 2007.

And Peter Bracken wound back the clock by wearing his first ever Connacht training jersey when he and his wife Rachel and their children travelled from their home in Castlebar.

"I went up to the attic to try and find a Connacht jersey and I found a few of them. But I decided I would go with the oldest one, the very first one. It was 2001 that I wore it last. It still fitted me but I suppose back then jerseys weren't tight fitting. But, unfortunately, 15 years later it is actually tight fitting.

"In my first year with Connacht our training jerseys were actually the playing jerseys from the year before. So that'll tell you what things were like. There was one set of jerseys for the year and then at the end of the

---

'But we were home before any of the fans. You get back to Galway and everyone you know that went by bus and by plane and boat, no one thought about 'What happens if we win?'

year they were used as a training jersey for the next year. That was the very first jersey I got handed to me on the first day I arrived in Connacht. There was no number on the back of it, but it has a special place for me. And that was the jersey I wore to the homecoming," said Bracken.

He said he was glad to get to Galway early as it was clear that a big crowd was gathering to welcome the team home.

"We got to the Sportsground about an hour before the lads took off to go to the starting point for the parade. We were just down on the training pitch and there was a massive crowd gathered already.

"A good few people recognised me from back in the day, but there were a lot more didn't know me. I suppose I met maybe 20 or 30 of the 500 or so that would have went to watch us play on a regular basis. But it was nice to get recognised all the same.

"I stayed around afterwards and bumped into a few of the current players, Locks (Ronan Loughney) and a few that I would have played with. I had a very quick chat with Pat Lam as well and congratulated him on it all," added Bracken.

By now the magnitude of the win was sinking in for the Connacht players and management, but John Muldoon said he will never forget the welcome afforded to them when they arrived back in Ireland West Airport in Knock with the Pro12 trophy in the early hours of Sunday morning.

Over 2,000 delighted fans were at the airport to greet the victorious squad when they touched down before 1am on their charter flight from Edinburgh.

The chairman of Mayo County Council, Cllr Michael Holmes, and the managing director of the airport Joe Gilmore, welcomed the victorious squad home.

By happy coincidence the airport had earlier that day staged a big charity race on the runway and the stage and public address system in place for that was then used when the Connacht team landed.

"It was a special night. Earlier that evening 2,000 people had participated in our charity runway run and then for so many people to come and welcome the team home was superb," said Donal Healy, head of marketing at the airport.

"And the Connacht players, management and officers were superb as well and they spent a lot of time with the fans."

Connacht president Gerry O'Donnell with Ronan Loughney

Bonfires blazed as the team bus was given a garda escort all the way to Galway. A newly married couple, Sheila Burke and Conor Mills, even left their wedding celebration at the Claregalway Hotel to greet the victorious squad.

"That's right! It was Claregalway we went through and we saw the bride and groom outside and loads of people waving. It was crazy! It was great to see," said Tiernan O'Halloran.

The tradition of bonfires might be familiar to O'Halloran and the other Irish lads but the likes of Aly Muldowney from Stafford in England was taken back by it.

"In England, we have Guy Fawkes Night so we have bonfires then. It was a new concept for me, the bonfires on the side of the road. I'd never seen that before for celebrations.

"Knock was unreal. We got off the plane, came out of the airport and there was a few thousand people there. That was pretty special.

"That was really good. When we got back to Galway a few boys went to a pub but I had to get back because I had to sort my cat out. The dogs were in kennels but the cat was in the house so I had to get back. It must have been four in the morning so I was just knackered physically and mentally anyway.

"But the next day, the celebrations started. When we went on the open-top bus, that was incredible. It felt like the whole of Connacht was there. We didn't think anyone would hardly be there because no-one would have been back from Edinburgh at that stage, apart from us. But there were thousands there, it was ridiculous, especially when there was such a crowd in Edinburgh. It was just unreal, the whole lot of it.

"I think for the past six months before that, even going out for lunch you'd have people coming up saying: 'we're so proud of you and what you're doing.' The whole town was buzzing for months because we were doing well in the league. The week after, we celebrated for the full week. It was just ridiculous, town was crazy," said Muldowney.

O'Halloran said that time just flew from the match finishing to being back in Galway, with everyone on a high after the win

"There were a few beers in the changing room after the match and then we went to the airport straight away. There were a few more beers in the airport but our plane was actually delayed. I think we were sitting on the runway for about 45 minutes until we took off. Bundee was at the top of the plane leading song after song. It was just crazy on the plane for pretty much two hours by the time we got back and then we got to the homecoming in Knock and a few thousand people were

Big welcome at Ireland West Airport in Knock

there at 2.30 in the morning, kids as well. It was crazy. By the time we got on the bus then, things had got a bit more quiet again. Lads were tired obviously after the game. It was really cool driving back. Pretty much every town had a bonfire."

The Mayor of Galway, Cllr Frank Fahy, said that the Connacht rugby team epitomised all that was good about the west of Ireland.

Cllr Fahy, who accompanied the team home from Edinburgh, said that the players and management had brought honour and glory to every corner of the province.

"It's not just rugby people who are celebrating. People from all sports and people with little interest in sport are walking a bit taller today.

"They have done it against all the odds and the manner in which they captured the Pro12 title was breathtaking. Everyone is so proud of them," he said.

Thousands lined the streets of Galway to give the squad and management a heroes' welcome as they took an open-top bus tour from the Town Hall to the Sportsground.

And even the notoriously wet city of Galway obliged with bright sunshine, providing the perfect backdrop to a historic occasion.

John Muldoon said what he couldn't understand was if there were that many people in Murrayfield, and they were hardly home by Sunday afternoon, who was going to come to welcome the team through the city streets?

"My defining moment was coming in off the bus outside Murrayfield and seeing all the Connacht fans in the stadium and on the steps up along. That will always stay with me, it's even giving me goose bumps now thinking of it again. That's definitely the biggest and best feeling that I have had ever in a jersey, or being a part of anything before, or probably for a long time again.

"In the changing room afterwards was something very, very special, so too was the journey home.

"But we were home before any of the fans. You get back to Galway and everyone you know that went by bus and by plane and boat, no one thought about 'What happens if we win?'

"There was a little bit of: 'Who the hell is going to show up in the Sportsground at 4 o'clock because no one is

WELCOME HOME...Thousands of people flood down College Road as John Muldoon and Ronan Loughney look on

WARNING
NO RIGHT TURN
AHEAD

home?' There was a slight bit of trepidation wondering if anyone was going to be at the Sportsground when we got here. But to see the crowd walking up College Road behind the bus was phenomenal.

"I was at the back of the bus with Ronan Loughney, Tiernan, Brownie, Aly, Finlay and Tom McCartney. There were a couple of Galway lads mixed in with a few foreigners and just to see the wave of people coming up College Road was phenomenal. Thinking about all the people, all the family members, all your friends that actually weren't here, you think: 'If they are all over there, who the hell are these people and where have they come out of?'

"That was a nice moment. Walking back up and to see the crowd coming behind us was pretty special," said Muldoon.

Thousands turned out to greet the team and many then followed the bus to the Sportsground. The players were shocked by the size of the crowd and Tiernan O'Halloran said it was a memory which will stay with them forever.

"I remember driving through Eyre Square and seeing the whole of Eyre Square filled. We drove all the way through town. Up College Road and we were just at the front gate of the Sportsground and you could look back towards Yeats' College and literally the whole of College Road was completely filled with people. And to see it from the top of the bus, it was unbelievable.

"We were taking photo after photo thinking we will never forget something like this. Back at the Sportsground and the whole pitch was filled for more speeches and things. It still hadn't sunk in what had happened. It had all happened so quickly," said O'Halloran.

Pat Lam, who had learned a few words of the Irish language as the season reached its climax, was given a massive ovation by the crowd who were waiting on the back pitch in the Sportsground.

Lam said it was an honour and privilege to work with such a dedicated group.

"We represent Galway, Mayo, Roscommon, Leitrim and Sligo – the five counties – and all the Connacht people living abroad, and we are honoured to do that.

"We are so grateful for all the support and goodwill we have received and we now want to build on this," he said.

The togetherness of the squad had been illustrated when the players put their hands in their pockets to bring four academy players over to Edinburgh, after Connacht put a limit on the number of players who could travel.

And the team spirit was also apparent a few weeks earlier when several players went to a dwelling in the city to demand the return of Robbie Henshaw's laptop after it was stolen from his car but was located using a tracking device.

The city opened its arms to the team as the celebrations went on for several days.

But Fionn Carr cut short the celebrations for a poignant reason.

"I was planning on spending a few days in Galway but I didn't actually because when I was in college I used to live with Devin Toner. Devin missed the final because his dad died. I went back and I went to the house to pay my respects to Dev and his family."

John Holland and his family, and Mick Grealish, had prepared the Sportsground for many an event down through the decades, but the homecoming trumped everything.

"It was the best day ever," said Grealish. "Sure none of us ever thought we would see a day like that. It's still hard to believe it happened."

Niyi Adeolokun and John Muldoon display the Pro12 trophy at the Sportsground

CHAPTER TWENTY FIVE
_The Future

One of Pat Lam's strengths is his ability to read a situation and pinpoint exactly where it fits in the overall scheme of things.

Rugby, like all other sports and, indeed, most things in life, tends to be cyclical, so it is important to be able to gauge the impact of events.

"Good times don't shape your character in any significant way," Lam said. "It's when things get tough that you develop as a person. It's been a difficult start to the season.

"No matter how much you might warn against complacency, the belief and the desire have to come from within. The boys expected things to happen for them this time around. You have to make things happen.

"We had huge motivation last season, and every season before that, in that the club had never won a trophy. Now the silverware was there, what next? We struggled for answers. We would all trot out the same phrases, do the same routines and were guilty of just going through the motions."

You would be forgiven for presuming those words were uttered in the opening weeks of the 2016-17 season when Connacht lost their first three games in the defence of their Pro12 crown.

But Lam made those comments in December 2000, just over six months after he captained Northampton Saints to win the Heineken Cup final against Munster.

Their hopes of retaining it were blown away when they lost all four of their opening pool matches.

Most sports, not just the professional ones, are like that. But the need to capitalise when you are on top is paramount, although clubs in a variety of sports have struggled to deal with victory.

Connacht always thrived with their 'chip on the shoulder' mentality. Most underdogs struggle when their fortunes change and they are fancied.

Lam, as a player, saw how Newcastle Falcons and then Northampton Saints did not handle success well. They didn't build on it.

The Pro12 win has probably removed the threat of disbandment forever, but after tasting the sweetness of glory, how will Connacht handle a bad spell? And given the cyclical nature of sport, it is inevitable that they will go through a rough patch, the same as the likes of

Munster will rise from their slumber of recent years.

But there has to be a legacy from the Pro12 win. The start of the 2016-17 season was disappointing, not just the results, although they picked up with the wins over Edinburgh and Ulster, with the Champions Cup victory over Toulouse providing great hope.

The absence of pre-season games and the fact that the homecoming celebration took place in the city while thousands of fans were still making their way home from Edinburgh, meant that the opening game of the new season against Glasgow Warriors was the first opportunity a lot of fans had to greet the team in Galway as champions.

Yet, the Sportsground wasn't full for that fixture, even with reduced capacity, while there was a distinct lack of fanfare. It was the opening game after Connacht won a trophy for the first time in their 131-year history, but even so it was all a bit flat.

You could understand management wanting to play it down, not wanting to carry celebrations into a new season, but you couldn't help but feel that the occasion demanded something more momentous.

The team itself will continue to evolve. Coaches and players will come and go, while the IRFU have seen a great return on their investment. They might have their critics but the reality is that when it came to the crunch, they backed Connacht in 2003 and 2009, and when they stepped that up in recent years it led to glory.

The key issue which has to be addressed with a degree of urgency is what to do with the Sportsground, or should Connacht consider going elsewhere?

The Sportsground, in its current form, has probably hit the maximum in terms of what it can deliver. In several of the reports which Morgan Buckley carried out for the IRFU in the first decade of professionalism, the need to develop modern stadiums was highlighted. That's what drove the decisions to redevelop Lansdowne Road, Thomond Park, Ravenhill and the RDS.

Connacht need to step up to the plate as well and if they don't – or can't – do it when they are Pro12 champions, when are they going to do it?

The co-tenancy with the Irish Greyhound Board is a complication, but there were similar issues with co-tenants in Lansdowne Road and Thomond Park and

SMILE!...Tiernan O'Halloran organises a selfie with students at Seamount College in Kinvara in south Co Galway in October 2016

they were eventually resolved.

It should also be acknowledged that, for years, the only covered accommodation and catering facilities available to supporters at the Sportsground, were provided by the Irish Greyhound Board, at no capital cost to Connacht. Imagine how grim the venue would be if it wasn't for the new stand built and paid for by the Irish Greyhound Board in 2003?

The location of the Sportsground is its biggest asset. Planning permission exists to add 800 seats on a second level in the Clan Stand.

Even if the greyhounds remain, could stands not be built behind the goals, extending over the track? Connacht don't need a huge increase in capacity, a 10-12,000 stadium would be sufficient, but they do need a modern facility which can generate income and, at the same time, offer comfortable viewing to supporters.

Bernard Jackman couldn't believe how much the Sportsground had changed from when he spent two spells there when he returned with his Grenoble side.

"I don't think it's ugly anymore. It's a little cauldron. There's a good atmosphere. When we were there, there were very few fans on the other side of the pitch and there were rarely fans behind the goals. But now, it's a real cauldron, it's a phenomenal place to play. I think if I was in Connacht again, I would love the Sportsground."

A successful bid to stage the 2023 Rugby World Cup in Ireland would probably see Pearse Stadium in Salthill utilised as a venue for games and that would initiate the playing of rugby at Galway's GAA headquarters, a habit which might be continued to facilitate big Connacht matches.

But the goodwill generated by the Pro12 win needs to be tapped into quickly, not least as Connacht is primarily a GAA region.

Players will now see a move to Connacht in a different light. John Muldoon pointed out before that some of his colleagues welcomed live television coverage as a chance to showcase their wares in the hope of being signed by other clubs.

The wages at Connacht have always been lower than other clubs. Even in areas like win bonuses, Connacht players picked them up less frequently, even though it is the same amount for all players in Ireland. In recent

The Sportsground in September 2016

times there is a win bonus to each of the matchday 23 of €500, while winning the Pro12 final netted €1,500 per man. There were some players in Connacht in the 2015-16 who picked up €10,000 in win bonuses during that season.

The international recognition which has followed Connacht's elevation is the key driver in players now considering coming to the Sportsground. A move west is no longer seen in desperation terms.

A few weeks into the 2015-16 season Ultan Dillane outlined in an interview how his housemate Eoghan Masterson had been called into the Irish Wolfhounds squad during the summer, and he had set himself a target of getting a similar call-up that season.

A few months later Dillane made his Irish senior debut in the Six Nations and by the end of the season Matt Healy, a player plucked from the All-Ireland League, was also capped.

The value to Connacht of these players being capped can't be underestimated, but another key factor in Connacht continuing to develop will be holding on to talent, especially from the other Irish provinces.

Michael Bradley watched a string of great young players head away after making the breakthrough at the Sportsground. He hopes the Pro12 win will ensure that this trend stops.

"Connacht still remains the only province that full internationals will actually move from within Ireland. You would like to think that Robbie Henshaw will be the last of them to move like that. No other Irish internationals move internally," said Bradley.

Jerry Flannery has seen at first hand how Munster have tried to rebuild following success. "What is difficult for Connacht now, going forward, the challenge they are going to have is how are they going to build on it. Are they going to be able to retain coaches and players? Guys are saying: 'I love Connacht' and the environment and so on. Well, if they do then they should stay there.

"Connacht may not win the Pro12 but they can't have a drop off. They need to be within touching distance. If they can stay there it can become very special.

"I looked at what we did with Munster on the field, everything was amazing. But then things started to drop off, we found it hard to get back to where we want.

Connacht are in a different position but they have to be careful about how they got forward. They have fantastic players and need to get those guys tied up."

Andrew Farley has seen how Grenoble, who rebuilt their club back up from the lower league after a financial crisis, since becoming a Top 14 outfit again, has dealt with legacy.

"I think every title is for everyone. When we won Pro D2, a good point that our coach Fabrice Landreau made was that we've got to remember the guys that won Federale 1 to get us to Pro D2.

"Connacht now have a trophy for the first time and that should help build a legacy, because a strong past can build a strong future. It is now a great opportunity for Connacht."

Billy Glynn is now back as president of Galwegians RFC after years spent battling for Connacht, and he is hopeful that the province can now prosper after their historic title win and he doesn't see the threat of disbandment ever arising again.

"Over the years we'd have a victory and then we'd have a defeat and we're weren't a threat to anyone. Probably what saved us was that we were unsuccessful. So therefore they could live with us.

"We're now a threat but we're a threat in a different way in the fact that we had five players capped for Ireland in one match and more followed in South Africa.

"They key thing now is to keep it going, and that should happen. There are great structures in place, we need to keep that.

"I'd be very reluctant to move out of the Sportsground, the location is brilliant. You'd have to have something that was marvellous before you'd move out of it.

"Players and coaches will come and go, that's the nature of the business. If you look at the successful soccer teams in the world, they refresh every year. We need to be able to do that as well. But it is a bright future, there is no doubt about that. It has come a long way," said Glynn.

It has been a fascinating journey for Glynn and all the many other people who shared it along the way...the despair, the worry, the anger, the frustration, and then the sheer joy of winning.

There were many of us back in that dark winter of 2002-03 who felt we were the ones with our hands on the candle when the flame would be extinguished forever.

Thankfully, Connacht survived and was allowed develop to prosper. Connacht – the team that refused to die.

YOUNG GUN...Conan O'Donnell is presented with his U-20 player of the year award by Pearse Keller of sponsors Keller Travel of Ballinasloe at the 2016 awards gala

■ ROUND 10

CONNACHT 3-10 ULSTER
Saturday December 26, 6pm, The Sportsground
Attendance: 5,876
Referee: Peter Fitzgibbon (IRFU)

SCORING SEQUENCE:
P Jackson pen 0-3; (HT 0-3); AJ MacGinty pen 3-3; N Williams try 3-8; P Jackson con 3-10.

CONNACHT: T O'Halloran; N Adeolokun, B Aki, C Ronaldson (R Parata 78), M Healy; J Carty (AJ MacGinty 57), K Marmion (I Porter 78); F Bealham (R Loughney 61), D Heffernan (S Delahunt 55), N White (R Ah You 69), U Dillane, A Muldowney (A Browne 57); J Muldoon (capt), J Connolly, E Masterson (S O'Brien 55).
ULSTER: L Ludik; A Trimble, L Marshall, S McCloskey, R Scholes; P Jackson, R Pienaar (P Marshall 69); A Warwick (C Black 44), R Herring (capt), W Herbst (R Lutton 51); A O'Connor (S Mulholland 71), F van der Merwe; R Diack, S Reidy (R Wilson 55), N Williams.

Ulster inflicted a first home defeat of the season on Connacht as Nick Williams' late try wrapped up the win. The game looked to be heading for a draw, but when Luke Marshall was stopped just short, Williams piled over for Ulster.

STANDINGS AFTER ROUND 10

Team	P	W	D	L	TB	TL	Pts
Scarlets	10	8	0	2	1	2	35
Connacht	10	7	0	3	3	3	34
Leinster	9	7	0	2	2	1	31
Ulster	10	6	0	4	4	3	31
Edinburgh Rugby	10	6	0	4	1	3	28
Munster	10	6	0	4	2	2	28
Glasgow Warriors	9	5	0	4	3	3	26
Ospreys	10	5	0	5	2	2	24
Cardiff Blues	10	3	0	7	2	4	18
Newport Gwent Dragons	10	3	0	7	0	3	15
Zebre	10	3	0	7	1	0	13
Benetton Treviso	10	0	0	10	0	7	7

■ ROUND 11

LEINSTER 13-0 CONNACHT
Friday January 1, 5pm, RDS Arena
Attendance: 14,297
Referee: George Clancy (IRFU)

SCORING SEQUENCE:
J Sexton pen 3-0; (HT 3-0); J van der Flier try 8-0; J Sexton con 10-0; I Madigan pen 13-0.

LEINSTER: R Kearney (Z Kirchner 74); F McFadden, G Ringrose, B Te'o, D Kearney; J Sexton (I Madigan 71), E Reddan (N McCarthy 75); J McGrath (P Dooley 70), R Strauss (J Tracy 61), M Moore (M Bent 70); D Toner, M McCarthy (R Molony 67); R Ruddock (capt), J van der Flier, J Murphy (S O'Brien 51).
CONNACHT: T O'Halloran (R Parata 74); N Adeolokun, B Aki, C Ronaldson, M Healy; J Carty (AJ MacGinty 64), K Marmion (I Porter 64); F Bealham (R Loughney 64), T McCartney, N White (R Ah You 9-14, 53); A Muldowney (U Dillane 61), A Browne; J Muldoon (capt), J Heenan (S O'Brien 51), E Masterson.

Connacht fell to a sixth straight Pro12 defeat in a row to Leinster at the RDS.
Pat Lam's side had never won at the Dublin venue but only trailed 3-0 with the wind at their backs after the break. But Leinster went through the gears and Josh van der Flier's try on the hour made the difference.

STANDINGS AFTER ROUND 11

Team	P	W	D	L	TB	TL	Pts
Scarlets	11	8	0	3	1	3	36
Leinster	10	8	0	2	2	1	35
Connacht	11	7	0	4	3	3	34
Edinburgh Rugby	11	7	0	4	1	3	32
Munster	11	7	0	4	2	2	32
Ulster	11	6	0	5	4	4	32
Ospreys	11	6	0	5	2	2	28
Glasgow Warriors	10	5	0	5	3	4	27
Cardiff Blues	11	4	0	7	3	4	23
Zebre	11	4	0	7	1	0	17
Newport Gwent Dragons	11	3	0	8	0	4	16
Benetton Treviso	11	0	0	11	0	7	7

■ ROUND 12

SCARLETS 21-19 CONNACHT
Sunday January 10, 2.30pm, Parc y Scarlets
Attendance: 5,888
Referee: Marius Mitrea (FIR)

SCORING SEQUENCE:
C Ronaldson pen 0-3; M Healy try 0-8; C Ronaldson con 0-10; A Thomas pen 3-10; (HT 3-10); A Thomas pen 6-10; S Evans try 11-10; A Thomas con 13-10; C Ronaldson pen 13-13; M Collins try 18-13; J Carty pen 18-16; J Carty pen 18-19; S Shingler pen 21-19.

SCARLETS: M Collins; S Evans, R King (S Hughes 67), H Parkes, DTH van der Merwe; A Thomas (S Shingler 72), A Davies (R Williams 54); R Evans, K Owens (capt), S Lee (R Jones 76); T Price, L Rawlins (M Paulino 72); A Shingler, J Barclay, M Allen.
CONNACHT: T O'Halloran; N Adeolokun, B Aki, C Ronaldson (R Parata 63), M Healy; J Carty, K Marmion (I Porter 76); F Bealham (R Loughney 67), T McCartney (D Heffernan 68), N White (R Ah You 67); U Dillane, A Browne (A Muldowney 9); J Muldoon (capt), J Heenan (S O'Brien 68), E Masterson.

Matt Healy bagged an early try for Connacht, but they were overtaken at the death as Steven Shingler kicked a last-minute penalty to take the win in this top of the table battle at Parc Y Scarlets.
Connacht led 10-0 early on, but could not add to Healy's try and slipped to a fifth league loss of the campaign.

STANDINGS AFTER ROUND 12

Team	P	W	D	L	TB	TL	Pts
Scarlets	12	9	0	3	1	3	40
Leinster	11	9	0	2	2	1	39
Edinburgh Rugby	12	8	0	4	1	3	36
Connacht	12	7	0	5	3	4	35
Munster	11	7	0	4	2	2	32
Ulster	11	6	0	5	4	4	32
Ospreys	12	6	0	6	2	2	28
Glasgow Warriors	10	5	0	5	3	4	27
Cardiff Blues	11	4	0	7	3	4	23
Zebre	11	4	0	7	1	0	17
Newport Gwent Dragons	11	3	0	8	0	4	16
Benetton Treviso	12	0	0	12	0	7	7

Masseur Robbie Fox, analyst Sean Mannion, kitman Martin Joyce, assistant kitman Philip Coyle and PR and media manager Louise Creedon

■ ROUND 13

CONNACHT 30-17 SCARLETS
Saturday January 30, 3pm, The Sportsground
Attendance: 5,292
Referee: Ben Whitehouse (WRU)

SCORING SEQUENCE:
J Carty pen 3-0; J Heenan try 8-0; J Heenan try 13-0; (HT 13-0); A Thomas pen 13-3; DTH van der Merwe try 13-8; A Thomas con 13-10; J Carty pen 16-10; D Buckley try 21-10; J Carty con 23-10; R Ah You try 28-10; J Carty con 30-10; G Owen try 30-15; A Thomas con 30-17.

CONNACHT: T O'Halloran; D Poolman, R Henshaw, B Aki, M Healy (R Parata 30); J Carty (C Ronaldson 65), C Blade (I Porter 74); D Buckley (R Loughney 67), T McCartney (D Heffernan 67), F Bealham (R Ah You 62); G Naoupu (U Dillane 58), A Muldowney; J Muldoon, J Heenan (J Connolly 65), E Masterson.
SCARLETS: L Williams (M Collins 62); T Williams (S Shingler 67), G Owen, H Parkes, DTH van der Merwe; A Thomas, R Williams; P John (D Evans 66), R Elias (K Myhill 66), R Jones (P Edwards 36); T Price, L Rawlins (J Jones 74); A Shingler, W Boyde, M Allen (D Evans 54-58).

Seldom has the battering power of a rampaging scrum been used with the precision Connacht displayed to get their Pro12 campaign back on track with a priceless win at the Sportsground.
The win, their first in the Pro12 since the historic win in Thomond Park in November, is probably the most significant in their best season of the professional era and set them up for a massive finish to the season.

STANDINGS AFTER ROUND 13

Team	P	W	D	L	TB	TL	Pts
Ulster	13	8	0	5	5	4	41
Scarlets	13	9	0	4	1	3	40
Connacht	13	8	0	5	4	4	40
Leinster	12	9	0	3	2	1	39
Edinburgh Rugby	13	8	0	5	1	4	37
Munster	12	8	0	4	2	2	36
Ospreys	13	6	1	6	2	2	30
Glasgow Warriors	11	5	1	5	3	4	29
Cardiff Blues	12	5	0	7	3	4	27
Newport Gwent Dragons	13	4	0	9	0	5	21
Zebre	12	4	0	8	1	1	18
Benetton Treviso	13	0	0	13	0	7	7

■ ROUND 14

NEWPORT GWENT DRAGONS 21-26 CONNACHT
Thursday February 11, 7.30pm, Rodney Parade
Attendance: 4,128
Referee: David Wilkinson (IRFU)

SCORING SEQUENCE:
J Tovey pen 3-0; M Healy try 3-5; C Ronaldson con 3-7; A Hughes try 8-7; T O'Halloran try 8-12; C Ronaldson con 8-14; A Hewitt try 13-14; A O'Brien con 15-14; (HT 15-14); A O'Brien pen 18-14; A O'Brien pen 21-14; E Masterson try 21-19; B Aki try 21-24; C Ronaldson con 21-26.

NEWPORT GWENT DRAGONS: G Rhys Jones; A Hewitt, A Hughes, A Warren, N Scott; J Tovey (A O'Brien 27), S Pretorius (C Davies 69); P Price (L Garrett 64), E Dee, B Harris (S Knight 64); M Screech (C Hill 67), R Landman (capt); B White (J Benjamin 74), N Cudd, N Crosswell.
CONNACHT: T O'Halloran; D Poolman (R Parata 68), B Aki, C Ronaldson, M Healy; A MacGinty (P Robb 80), C Blade (K Marmion 45); B Buckley, T McCartney, R Ah You (F Bealham 45); A Muldowney, G Naoupu (U Dillane 55); J Muldoon (capt), J Heenan (E McKeon 63), E Masterson.

It's taken two and a half months to get back to the top, but Connacht pulled level with the Pro12 leaders thanks to their bonus point win in Newport.
Tries from Matt Healy, Tiernan O'Halloran, Eoghan Masterson and Bundee Aki sealed the win as Pat Lam's side drew level with Ulster on top of the standings.

STANDINGS AFTER ROUND 14

Team	P	W	D	L	TB	TL	Pts
Ulster	14	9	0	5	5	4	45
Connacht	14	9	0	5	5	4	45
Leinster	13	10	0	3	3	1	44
Scarlets	14	10	0	4	1	3	44
Edinburgh Rugby	14	8	0	6	1	5	38
Munster	13	8	0	5	2	3	37
Ospreys	14	7	1	6	2	2	34
Glasgow Warriors	12	5	1	6	3	5	30
Cardiff Blues	13	5	0	8	3	5	28
Newport Gwent Dragons	14	4	0	10	0	6	22
Zebre	13	4	0	9	1	1	18
Benetton Treviso	14	1	0	13	0	7	11

■ ROUND 15

ZEBRE 34-51 CONNACHT
Saturday February 20, 5.30pm,
Stadio Sergio Lanfranchi
Attendance: 1,850
Referee: Gary Conway (IRFU)

SCORING SEQUENCE:
C Ronaldson pen 0-3; K Haimona pen 3-3; M Healy try 3-8; C Ronaldson con 3-10; K Haimona pen 6-10; K Marmion try 6-15; C Ronaldson con 6-17; J Meyer try 11-17; K Haimona con 13-17; (HT 13-17); M Healy try 13-22; C Ronaldson con 13-24; K Haimona try 18-24; K Haimona con 20-24; M Healy try 20-29; C Ronaldson con 20-31; D van Schalkwyk try 25-31; K Haimona con 27-31; N Adeolokun try 27-36; AJ MacGinty con 27-38; AJ MacGinty pen 27-41; N Adeolokun try 27-46; AJ MacGinty con 27-48; F Ruzza try 32-48; K Haimona con 34-48; A MacGinty pen 34-51.

ZEBRE: M Muliaina (U Beyers 51); G Toniolatti, G Bisegni (T Boni 57), M Pratichetti, K Van Zyl; K Haimona, L Burgess (M Panunzi 68); B Postiglioni (A De Marchi 57), O Fabiani (E Coria 75), D Chistolini (P Ceccarelli 56); G Koegelenberg, M Bortolami; E Caffini, J Meyer (F Ruzza 56), D Van Schalkwyk (F Cristiano 66).
CONNACHT: T O'Halloran (D Poolman 67); N Adeolokun, B Aki, C Ronaldson (P Robb 50), M Healy; AJ MacGinty, K Marmion (C Blade 60); D Buckley (R Loughney 60), T McCartney, F Bealham (R Ah You 60); B Marshall (D Heffernan 61), A Muldowney; J Muldoon, J Heenan (E Masterson 26, G Naoupu 46), E McKeon.

Matt Healy did his Ireland aspirations no harm at all with a hat-trick, but Pat Lam's side were left counting the cost of victory in Parma as his injury-battered side took a bonus point win.
Healy and Kieran Marmion crossed in the first-half before Healy ran in another two in the first eight minutes after the break.

STANDINGS AFTER ROUND 15

Team	P	W	D	L	TB	TL	Pts
Connacht	15	10	0	5	6	4	50
Leinster	14	11	0	3	3	1	48
Scarlets	15	11	0	4	1	3	48
Ulster	15	9	0	6	5	5	46
Edinburgh Rugby	15	8	0	7	1	5	38
Ospreys	15	8	1	6	2	2	38
Munster	14	8	0	6	2	4	38
Glasgow Warriors	13	6	1	6	4	5	35
Cardiff Blues	14	5	0	9	3	6	27
Newport Gwent Dragons	15	4	0	11	0	7	23
Zebre	14	4	0	10	2	1	19
Benetton Treviso	15	2	0	13	0	7	15

Academy players Sean O'Brien, Rory Parata, Rory Moloney, Peter Robb, Shane Delahunt, Conor McKeon, Saba Meunargia, Conan O'Donnell, Ciaran Gaffney and Cormac Brennan

ROUND 16

CONNACHT 30-22 OSPREYS
Saturday February 27, 7.35pm, The Sportsground
Attendance: 5,279
Referee: George Clancy (IRFU)

SCORING SEQUENCE:
B Aki try 5-0; C Ronaldson con 7-0; S Davies pen 7-3; AJ MacGinty try 12-3; C Ronaldson con 14-3; B John try 14-8; D Baker try 14-13; S Davies con 14-15; C Ronaldson pen 17-15; (HT 17-15); M Healy try 22-15; C Ronaldson con 24-15; R Webb try 24-20; S Davies con 24-22; C Ronaldson pen 27-22; C Ronaldson pen 30-22.

CONNACHT: T O'Halloran; N Adeolokun (D Poolman 63), B Aki, C Ronaldson (P Robb 76), M Healy; AJ MacGinty, C Blade (K Marmion 32); D Buckley (R Loughney 72), T McCartney (D Heffernan 73), R Ah You (F Bealham 58); B Marshall (D Qualter 41), A Muldowney; S O'Brien, J Heenan, G Naoupu (J Connolly 63).
OSPREYS: D Evans; J Hassler, JJ Engelbrecht (O Watkin 8), J Matavesi, B John (E Waker 68); S Davies, R Webb (B Leonard 73); P James (G Thomas 65), S Parry (S Otten 63), D Arhip (A Jarvis 52); J King, R Thornton; J Bearman (R Bernardo 52), O Cracknell, D Baker.

Matt Healy made it four tries in a week as Connacht's scintillating form continued with this win over Ospreys at the Sportsground. The league leaders denied Ospreys a losing bonus point as Bundee Aki, AJ MacGinty and Healy all crossed the whitewash, while Craig Ronaldson kicked 15 points.

STANDINGS AFTER ROUND 16

Team	P	W	D	L	TB	TL	Pts
Connacht	16	11	0	5	6	4	54
Leinster	15	12	0	3	4	1	53
Scarlets	16	11	0	5	1	4	49
Ulster	16	9	0	7	5	5	46
Edinburgh Rugby	16	9	0	7	1	5	42
Munster	15	9	0	6	2	4	42
Glasgow Warriors	14	7	1	6	4	5	39
Ospreys	16	8	1	7	2	2	38
Cardiff Blues	15	6	0	9	3	6	33
Newport Gwent Dragons	16	4	0	12	0	8	24
Zebre	15	4	0	11	2	1	19
Benetton Treviso	16	2	0	14	0	8	16

ROUND 17

EDINBURGH 23-28 CONNACHT
Friday March 4, 7.35pm, BT Murrayfield
Attendance: 3,584
Referee: Ben Whitehouse (WRU)

SCORING SEQUENCE:
AJ MacGinty try 0-5; C Ronaldson con 0-7; J Heenan try 0-12; C Ronaldson con 0-14; (HT 0-14); C Dean try 5-14; B Aki try 5-19; C Ronaldson con 5-21; D Hoyland try 10-21; S Hidalgo-Clyne con 12-21; C du Preez try 17-21; S Hidalgo-Clyne pen 20-21; E McKeon try 20-26; AJ MacGinty con 20-28; S Hidalgo-Clyne pen 23-28.

EDINBURGH: B Cochrane; D Hoyland, C Dean, M Scott (S Beard 23), T Brown; P Burleigh, S Hidalgo-Clyne; R Sutherland (A Dell 48), N Cochrane, J Andress (S Berghan 40); A Bresler (A Toolis 69), B Toolis; J Ritchie, H Watson, C Du Preez.
CONNACHT: T O'Halloran; D Poolman, B Aki, C Ronaldson (P Robb 70), M Healy; A J MacGinty, K Marmion (C Blade 69); D Buckley, T McCartney (D Heffernan 75), N White (R Ah You 40); Q Roux, (D Qualter 68) A Muldowney; S O'Brien (E McKeon 69), J Heenan, J Muldoon.

**Connacht replacement No 8 Eoin McKeon bagged the bonus point try as the league leaders made it five Pro12 wins in a row at Edinburgh.
AJ MacGinty, Jake Heenan and Bundee Aki touched down the other efforts as Connacht moved one step closer to securing Champions Cup rugby for next term at Murrayfield.**

STANDINGS AFTER ROUND 17

Team	P	W	D	L	TB	TL	Pts
Connacht	17	12	0	5	7	4	59
Leinster	17	13	0	4	4	2	58
Scarlets	17	12	0	5	1	4	53
Ulster	17	10	0	7	6	5	51
Munster	17	10	0	7	3	4	47
Glasgow Warriors	16	9	1	6	4	5	47
Edinburgh Rugby	17	9	0	8	1	6	43
Ospreys	17	8	1	8	2	3	39
Cardiff Blues	17	7	0	10	4	7	39
Newport Gwent Dragons	17	4	0	13	0	8	24
Zebre	16	4	0	12	2	1	19
Benetton Treviso	17	2	0	15	0	8	16

ROUND 18

CONNACHT 7-6 LEINSTER
Saturday March 26, 5.15pm, The Sportsground
Attendance: 7,300
Referee: Nigel Owens (WRU)

SCORING SEQUENCE:
K Marmion try 5-0; AJ MacGinty con 7-0; (HT 7-0); I Madigan pen 7-3; I Madigan pen 7-6.

CONNACHT: T O'Halloran (C Blade 66-71); N Adeolokun, B Aki, P Robb (R Henshaw 48), M Healy; AJ MacGinty (S O'Leary 61), K Marmion (Blade 74); D Buckley (R Loughney 70), T McCartney (D Heffernan 70), N White (F Bealham 6); Q Roux (A Browne 50), A Muldowney; S O'Brien (J Connolly 66), E McKeon, J Muldoon.
LEINSTER: I Nacewa; F McFadden, G Ringrose, B Te'o, L Fitzgerald (Z Kirchner 38); I Madigan, L McGrath (E Reddan 61); C Healy (J McGrath 47), R Strauss (S Cronin 50), T Furlong (M Ross 61); R Molony, H Triggs (D Toner 61); R Ryan, J van der Flier, R Ruddock (J Heaslip 66).

The Sportsground exploded at the full-time whistle as Connacht held out to beat Leinster, pulling further clear at the top of the Pro12 table thanks to Kieran Marmion's first-half try. Two Ian Madigan penalties for Leinster had threatened to upset the home side at the death, but after a series of five-metre scrums for the visitors, Connacht forced the turnover and ran down the clock for victory.

STANDINGS AFTER ROUND 18

Team	P	W	D	L	TB	TL	Pts
Connacht	18	13	0	5	7	4	63
Leinster	18	13	0	5	4	3	59
Scarlets	18	13	0	5	1	4	57
Munster	18	11	0	7	4	4	52
Ulster	18	10	0	8	6	5	51
Glasgow Warriors	17	10	1	6	4	5	51
Edinburgh Rugby	18	10	0	8	1	6	47
Cardiff Blues	18	8	0	10	5	7	44
Ospreys	18	8	1	9	2	3	39
Newport Gwent Dragons	18	4	0	14	0	9	25
Zebre	17	4	0	13	2	1	19
Benetton Treviso	18	2	0	16	0	8	16

LOCKS...Andrew Browne, Ultan Dillane and Aly Muldowney

■ ROUND 19

ULSTER 18-10 CONNACHT
Friday April 1, 7.35pm, Kingspan Stadium
Attendance: 16,224
Referee: Dudley Phillips (IRFU).

SCORING SEQUENCE:
P Jackson pen 3-0; P Jackson pen 6-0; R Best try 11-0; S O'Leary pen 11-3; (HT 11-3); C Gilroy try 16-3; P Jackson con 18-3; C Blade try 18-8; S O'Leary con 18-10.

ULSTER: J Payne; A Trimble, L Marshall (Cave 60), S McCloskey (S Olding 75), C Gilroy; P Jackson, R Pienaar (P Marshall 65); C Black, R Best (capt) (R Herring 64-70), R Lutton (C Ross 77); P Browne (R Diack 53), F van der Merwe; I Henderson (Herring 78), C Henry (S Reidy 46), R Wilson.
CONNACHT: R Henshaw; N Adeolokun (D Poolman 47), B Aki, P Robb, M Healy; S O'Leary, J Cooney (C Blade 47); D Buckley (R Loughney 71), T McCartney, R Ah You (F Bealham 42); A Browne, A Muldowney (U Dillane 42); J Muldoon (capt), J Connolly, E McKeon.

Connacht suffered a first defeat since January and failed to win a bonus point in Belfast as Leinster took over at the top of the Pro12 standings.
Caolin Blade's try gave Connacht some hope, but late sin-binnings for Shane O'Leary and Sean O'Brien saw the brave Connacht challenge falter.

STANDINGS AFTER ROUND 19

Team	P	W	D	L	TB	TL	Pts
Leinster	19	14	0	5	4	3	63
Connacht	19	13	0	6	7	4	63
Glasgow Warriors	19	12	1	6	6	5	61
Scarlets	19	13	0	6	1	5	58
Ulster	19	11	0	8	6	5	55
Munster	19	11	0	8	4	5	53
Edinburgh Rugby	19	11	0	8	2	6	52
Cardiff Blues	19	9	0	10	5	7	48
Ospreys	19	9	1	9	3	3	44
Newport Gwent Dragons	19	4	0	15	0	10	26
Zebre	19	4	0	15	2	1	19
Benetton Treviso	19	2	0	17	0	8	16

Analysts Conor McPhillips and Sean Mannion

■ ROUND 20

CONNACHT 35-14 MUNSTER
Saturday April 16, 7.15pm, The Sportsground
Attendance: 7,786
Referee: Ben Whitehouse (WRU)

SCORING SEQUENCE:
S O'Leary pen 3-0; S Zebo try 3-5; J Holland con 3-7; S O'Leary pen 6-7; M Sherry try 6-12; J Holland con 6-14; N Adeolokun try 11-14; S O'Leary con 13-14; Pen try 18-14; S O'Leary con 20-14; (HT 20-14); N Adeolokun try 25-14; F Bealham try 30-14; S O'Leary con 32-14; S O'Leary pen 35-14.

CONNACHT: R Henshaw; N Adeolokun, B Aki (F Carr 68), P Robb (J Carty 74), M Healy; S O'Leary, K Marmion (J Cooney 67); D Buckley (R Loughney 74), T McCartney (J Harris-Wright 74), F Bealham (JP Cooney 68); U Dillane, A Muldowney (A Browne 64); S O'Brien (J Connolly 72), E McKeon, J Muldoon (captain).
MUNSTER: S Zebo; D Sweetnam (A Conway 55), F Saili, R Scannell, K Earls; J Holland (I Keatley 65); C Murray; J Cronin (D Kilcoyne 55), M Sherry (N Scannell 55), S Archer (J Ryan 69); D Ryan (J Coghlan 69), B Holland; CJ Stander (captain), T O'Donnell, J O'Donoghue (D Kilcoyne 39-43, R Copeland 56).

Niyi Adeolokun bagged two tries as Connacht sealed their Champions Cup berth with a convincing bonus-point victory over a shell-shocked Munster at a bouncing Sportsground. For the second week in a row the winger ran in a brace in their second win of the season over their neighbours, as they took a huge step towards a home semi-final in the Pro12 – one more point will clinch a place in the last four for Pat Lam's side.

STANDINGS AFTER ROUND 20

Team	P	W	D	L	TB	TL	Pts
Leinster	20	15	0	5	5	3	68
Connacht	20	14	0	6	8	4	68
Glasgow Warriors	20	13	1	6	7	5	66
Ulster	20	12	0	8	7	5	60
Scarlets	20	13	0	7	1	5	58
Edinburgh Rugby	20	11	0	9	2	7	53
Munster	20	11	0	9	4	5	53
Cardiff Blues	20	10	0	10	5	7	52
Ospreys	20	10	1	9	4	3	49
Newport Gwent Dragons	20	4	0	16	0	10	26
Zebre	20	4	0	16	2	1	19
Benetton Treviso	20	2	0	18	0	8	16

■ ROUND 21

BENETTON TREVISO 22-21 CONNACHT
Friday April 29, 7.30pm, Stadio Monigo
Attendance: 3,700
Referee: Peter Fitzgibbon (IRFU)

SCORING SEQUENCE:
R Parata try 0-5; J Cooney con 0-7; F Carr try 0-12; J Cooney con 0-14; L Morisi try 5-14; B Steyn try 10-14; J Hayward con 12-14; (HT 12-14); Pen try 17-14; J Hayward con 19-14; P Robb try 19-19; J Cooney con 19-21; J Hayward pen 22-21.

BENETTON TREVISO: J Hayward, A Esposito, L Morisi (T Iannone 27), A Sgarbi, L Nitoglia (A Lucchese 68); S Christie (L McLean 17), E Gori; M Zanusso, O Gega (D Giazzon 71); S Ferrari (M Salesi 68); F Paulo, T Palmer (M Fuser 54); F Minto, A Zanni, A Steyn (M Lazzaroni 71).
CONNACHT: T O'Halloran; N Adeolokun, R Parata (R Henshaw 51), P Robb, F Carr; J Carty (AJ MacGinty 51); J Cooney (C Blade 68); R Loughney (F Bealham 46); T McCartney (D Heffernan 79), R Ah You (JP Cooney 59); Q Roux (A Muldowney 68), A Browne; S O'Brien, J Heenan (J Muldoon 58), E McKeon.

Connacht claimed their first Pro12 semi-final slot despite losing away to Treviso, thanks to Jayden Hayward's last-minute penalty.
Rory Parata and Fionn Carr both crossed early on to suggest an easy win for Connacht, but they were out-muscled from there and succumbed to a deserved win for the home side.

STANDINGS AFTER ROUND 21

Team	P	W	D	L	TB	TL	Pts
Glasgow Warriors	21	14	1	6	8	5	71
Connacht	21	14	0	7	8	5	69
Leinster	21	15	0	6	5	3	68
Ulster	21	13	0	8	7	5	64
Scarlets	21	14	0	7	2	5	63
Munster	21	12	0	9	5	5	58
Ospreys	21	11	1	9	5	3	54
Edinburgh Rugby	21	11	0	10	2	7	53
Cardiff Blues	21	10	0	11	5	7	52
Newport Gwent Dragons	21	4	0	17	0	10	26
Benetton Treviso	21	3	0	18	0	8	20
Zebre	21	4	0	17	2	1	19

AJ MacGinty and Peter Robb

■ ROUND 22

CONNACHT 14-7 GLASGOW WARRIORS
Saturday May 7, 3pm, The Sportsground
Attendance: 7,786
Referee: Ian Davies (WRU)

SCORING SEQUENCE:
B Aki try 5-0; AJ MacGinty con 7-0; (HT 7-0); G Reid try 7-5; F Russell con 7-7; T O'Halloran try 12-7; S O'Leary con 14-7.

CONNACHT: T O'Halloran; N Adeolokun, R Henshaw, B Aki (P Robb 74), M Healy; AJ MacGinty (S O'Leary 54), K Marmion (J Cooney 66); R Loughney, T McCartney, F Bealham (R Ah You 3, JP Cooney 52, Q Roux 70); U Dillane (Q Roux 73), A Muldowney; S O'Brien (E McKeon 63), J Heenan, J Muldoon (capt).
GLASGOW WARRIORS: S Hogg; T Seymour, A Dunbar (M Bennett 12), P Horne, L Jones; F Russell, A Price (G Hart 70), G Reid (J Yanuyanutawa 57), F Brown (P MacArthur 58), S Puafisi; L Nakarawa, J Gray (T Swinson 27-34); R Harley (Z Fagerson 56), R Wilson (S Favaro 19-27, 67), J Strauss.

Tries from Bundee Aki and Tiernan O'Halloran saw Connacht earn a home semi-final in the Pro12, settting up a rematch with Glasgow Warriors once again.
Warriors played the last 31 minutes with 14 men after tighthead prop Sila Puafisi was shown a straight red card, but even so Pat Lam's side were good value for the win at the Sportsground.

STANDINGS AFTER ROUND 22

Team	P	W	D	L	TB	TL	Pts
Leinster	22	16	0	6	6	3	73
Connacht	22	15	0	7	8	5	73
Glasgow Warriors	22	14	1	7	8	6	72
Ulster	22	14	0	8	8	5	69
Scarlets	22	14	0	8	2	5	63
Munster	22	13	0	9	6	5	63
Cardiff Blues	22	11	0	11	5	7	56
Ospreys	22	11	1	10	6	3	55
Edinburgh Rugby	22	11	0	11	2	8	54
Newport Gwent Dragons	22	4	0	18	0	10	26
Zebre	22	5	0	17	3	1	24
Benetton Treviso	22	3	0	19	0	8	20

■ SEMI-FINAL

CONNACHT 16-11 GLASGOW WARRIORS
Saturday May 21, 6.30pm, The Sportsground
Attendance: 7,800
Referee: Marius Mitrea (FIR)

SCORING SEQUENCE:
AJ MacGinty pen 3-0; D Weir pen 3-3; N Adeolokun try 8-3; AJ MacGinty con 10-3; (HT 10-3); L Nakarawa try 10-8; AJ MacGinty pen 13-8; D Weir pen 13-11; AJ MacGinty pen 16-11.

CONNACHT: T O'Halloran; N Adeolokun, R Henshaw, B Aki (P Robb 72), M Healy; AJ MacGinty, K Marmion (J Cooney 60); R Loughney (R Ah You 65), T McCartney, F Bealham (D Heffernan 71), U Dillane (A Browne 61), A Muldowney; E McKeon (S O'Brien 61), J Heenan (JP Cooney 74), J Muldoon (capt).
GLASGOW WARRIORS: S Hogg; T Seymour, M Bennett, P Horne (T Naiyaravoro 60), S Lamont; F Russell (D Hogg 1), H Pyrgos; G Reid (R Grant 63), F Brown (P MacArthur 60), Z Fagerson (D Rae 1, R Grant 60-63); L Nakarawa, J Gray (capt); R Wilson, S Favaro (A Ashe 30), J Strauss (T Swinson 67).

Captain John Muldoon rejoiced as Connacht made history and reached their first ever Pro12 final with a hard fought victory over reigning champions Glasgow at the Sportsground.
It was their second victory in three weeks against the Warriors and the first time in their 131-year history that Connacht found themselves just 80 minutes from silverware.

■ FINAL

CONNACHT 20-10 LEINSTER
Saturday May 28, 5.30pm, BT Murrayfield
Attendance: 34,550
Referee: Nigel Owens (WRU)

SCORING SEQUENCE:
T O'Halloran try 5-0; AJ MacGinty con 7-0; N Adeolokun try 12-0; AJ MacGinty pen 15-0; (HT 15-0); J Sexton pen 15-3; M Healy try 20-3; S Cronin try 20-8; J Sexton con 20-10.

CONNACHT: T O'Halloran (S O'Leary 69-72); N Adeolokun, R Henshaw, B Aiki, M Healy; AJ MacGinty, K Marmion (J Cooney 61, P Robb 66); R Loughney (R Ah You 69), T McCartney (D Heffernan 72), F Bealham; U Dillane (A Browne 62), A Muldowney; E McKeon (S O'Brien h-t), J Heenan, J Muldoon (capt).
LEINSTER: R Kearney (Z Kirchner 61); D Kearney (I Madigan 76), G Ringrose, B Te'o, L Fitzgerald; J Sexton, E Reddan (L McGrath 58); J McGrath, R Strauss (S Cronin 42), M Ross (T Furlong 42); R Molony (J Conan 62), M Kearney (H Triggs 17); R Ruddock, J Murphy, J Heaslip (capt).

Connacht are Pro12 champions for the first time after a stylish triumph over Leinster at Murrayfield.
Tries from Tiernan O'Halloran, Niyi Adeolokun and Matt Healy wrapped up the historic win for Pat Lam's side, who were by far the better team – despite a Sean Cronin-led fightback from Leo Cullen's charges.

8
JOHN
MULDOON

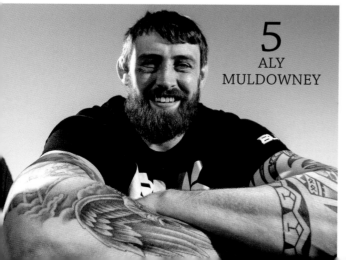

5
ALY
MULDOWNEY

4
ULTAN
DILLANE

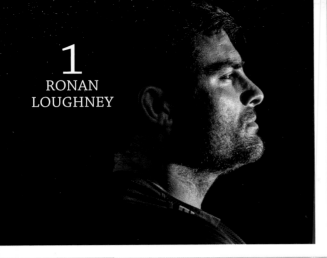

1
RONAN
LOUGHNEY

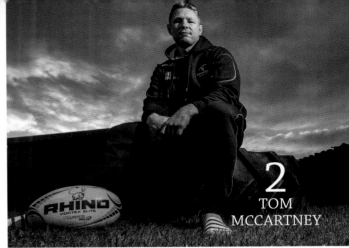

2
TOM
MCCARTNEY

3
FINLAY
BEALHAM

9
KIERAN
MARMION

6
EOIN
MCKEON

7

JAKE
HEENAN

10

AJ
MACGINTY

11
MATT
HEALY

12
BUNDEE
AKI

15
TIERNAN
O'HALLORAN

14
NIYI
ADEOLOKUN

13
ROBBIE
HENSHAW

CHAPTER TWENTY EIGHT
Results (1996-2016)

1996

DATE	MATCH	VENUE	COMPETITION
Sat 12th Oct 1996	Connacht 34-12 Petrarca	Sportsground	European Conference
Wed 16th Oct 1996	Dunvant 26-9 Connacht	Broadacre	European Conference
Sat 19th Oct 1996	Connacht 11-31 Northampton Saints	Sportsground	European Conference
Sun 27th Oct 1996	RC Toulon 44-10 Connacht	Stade Felix Mayol	European Conference
Sat 2nd Nov 1996	Connacht 30-18 Orell	Sportsground	European Conference

1997

DATE	MATCH	VENUE	COMPETITION
Tues 9th Sept 1997	Connacht 43-13 Northampton Saints	Sportsground	European Conference
Sun 14th Sept 1997	Nice 20-16 Connacht	Stade du Ray	European Conference
Sat 20th Sept 1997	Bordeaux-Begles 9-15 Connacht	Stade Andre Moga	European Conference
Sat 27th Sept 1997	Connacht 28-25 Nice	Sportsground	European Conference
Sat 4th Oct 1997	Connacht 22-15 Bordeaux-Begles	Sportsground	European Conference
Sat 11th Oct 1997	Northampton Saints 15-20 Connacht	Franklin's Gardens	European Conference
Sat 8th Nov 1997	Agen 40-27 Connacht	Stade Armandie	European Conference Quarter-final

1998

DATE	MATCH	VENUE	COMPETITION
Sat 26th Sept 1998	Newport 12-31 Connacht	Rodney Parade	European Shield
Wed 7th Oct 1998	Connacht 29-28 Perigueux	Sportground	European Shield
Sun 11th Oct 1998	Rugby Rovigo 20-21 Connacht	Stadio Mario Battaglini	European Shield
Sat 17th Oct 1998	Connacht 26-38 Narbonne	Sportsground	European Shield
Sat 31st Oct 1998	Caerphilly 39-8 Connacht	Virginia Park	European Shield
Sat 7th Nov 1998	Connacht 14-19 Racing Club de France	Sportsground	European Shield

1999-00

DATE	MATCH	VENUE	COMPETITION
Fri 19th Nov 1999	Ebbw Vale 32-9 Connacht	Eugene Cross Park	European Shield
Sun 27th Nov 1999	Steau Bucharest 30-20 Connacht	Club of Army	European Shield
Sat 11th Dec 1999	Connacht 27-13 RC Toulon	Sportsground	European Shield
Sat 18th Dec 1999	RC Toulon 41-15 Connacht	Stade Felix Mayo	European Shield
Sat 8th Jan 2000	Connacht 41-7 Steaua Bucharest	Sportsground	European Shield
Sat 15th Jan 2000	Connacht 19-42 Ebbw Vale	Sportsground	European Shield

2000-01

DATE	MATCH	VENUE	COMPETITION
Sat 7th Oct 2000	Connacht 14-16 Beziers	Sportsground	European Shield
Sat 14th Oct 2000	Neath 45-0 Connacht	The Gnoll	European Shield
Sun 22nd Oct 2000	AS Montferrand 58-21 Connacht	Stade Marcel Michelin	European Shield
Sat 28th Oct 2000	Connacht 3-12 AS Montferrand	Sportsground	European Shield
Sat 13th Jan 2001	Beziers 10-9 Connacht	Stade de la Méditerranée	European Shield
Sat 20th Jan 2001	Connacht 13-11 Neath	Sportsground	European Shield

2001-02

DATE	MATCH	VENUE	COMPETITION
Sat 18th Aug 2001	Cardiff Rugby 3-6 Connacht	Cardiff Arms Park	Celtic League
Fri 24th Aug 2001	Connacht 21-30 Edinburgh Rugby	Sportsground	Celtic League
Tues 28th Aug 2001	Munster Rugby 40-19 Connacht	Thomond Park	Celtic League
Fri 7th Sept 2001	Connacht 28-10 Neath	Sportsground	Celtic League
Tues 11th Sept 2001	Newport 14-16 Connacht	Rodney Parade	Celtic League
Sun 16th Sept 2001	Connacht 62-0 Caerphilly	Sportsground	Celtic League
Fri 28th Sept 2001	Connacht 18-6 Narbonne	Ericsson Park	Parker Pen Shield
Sat 6th Oct 2001	Rugby Roma 10-20 Connacht	Stade Tre Fontane	Parker Pen Shield
Sat 27th Oct 2001	Connacht 30-33 Sale Sharks	Sportsground	Parker Pen Shield
Sat 3rd Nov 2001	Sale Sharks 44-6 Connacht	Heywood Park	Parker Pen Shield
Sat 1st Dec 2001	Connacht 29-34 Glasgow Rugby	Sportsground	Celtic League Quarter-final
Sat 5th Jan 2002	Connacht 61-13 Rugby Roma	Sportsground	Parker Pen Shield
Sat 12th Jan 2002	Narbonne 34-22 Connacht	Parc de sport et de l'Amitie	Parker Pen Shield

2002-03

DATE	MATCH	VENUE	COMPETITION
Fri 30th Aug 2002	The Borders 27-28 Connacht	Selkirk	Celtic League
Fri 6th Sept 2002	Connacht 23-22 Cardiff Rugby	Sportsground	Celtic League
Fri 13th Sept 2002	Leinster Rugby 23-26 Connacht	Donnybrook	Celtic League
Fri 20th Sept 2002	Connacht 18-12 Newport	Sportsground	Celtic League
Sat 28th Sept 2002	Bridgend 23-24 Connacht	Brewery Field	Celtic League
Sat 5th Oct 2002	Connacht 0-40 Pontypridd	Sportsground	Celtic League
Sat 12th Oct 2002	Mont de Marsan 12-26 Connacht	Stade Guy Boniface	Parker Pen Challenge Cup
Sat 19th Oct 2002	Connacht 47-29 Mont de Marsan	Sportsground	Parker Pen Challenge Cup
Fri 25th Oct 2002	Glasgow Rugby 29-7 Connacht	Hughenden	Celtic League
Fri 29th Nov 2002	Munster Rugby 33-3 Connacht	Musgrave Park	Celtic League Quarter-final
Sat 7th Dec 2002	Narbonne 42-27 Connacht	Parc de Sport et de l'Amitie	Parker Pen Challenge Cup
Sun 15th Dec 2002	Connacht 23-7 Narbonne	Sportsground	Parker Pen Challenge Cup
Sat 11th Jan 2003	Connacht 30-35 Pontypridd	Dubarry Park	Parker Pen Challenge Cup Quarter-final
Sat 18th Jan 2003	Pontypridd 12-9 Connacht	Sardis Road	Parker Pen Challenge Cup Quarter-final

2003-04

DATE	MATCH	VENUE	COMPETITION
Sat 6th Sept 2003	Connacht 11-3 Edinburgh Rugby	Sportsground	Celtic League
Sat 13th Sept 2003	Cardiff Blues 33-17 Connacht	Cardiff Arms Park	Celtic League
Fri 26th Sept 2003	Glasgow Rugby 19-30 Connacht	Hughenden	Celtic League
Sat 11th Oct 2003	Connacht 42-19 The Borders	Sportsground	Celtic League
Fri 17th Oct 2003	Leinster Rugby 21-6 Connacht	Donnybrook	Celtic League
Fri 24th Oct 2003	Connacht 20-25 Llanelli Scarlets	Dubarry Park	Celtic League
Fri 31st Oct 2003	Ospreys 22-33 Connacht	St. Helen's	Celtic League
Sat 8th Nov 2003	Connacht 31-20 Ulster	Sportsground	Celtic League
Sun 23rd Nov 2003	Newport Gwent Dragons 28-19 Connacht	Rodney Parade	Celtic League
Sun 7th Dec 2003	Beziers 10-18 Connacht	Stade de la Méditerranée	Parker Pen Challenge Cup
Sat 13th Dec 2003	Connacht 11-13 Beziers	Sportsground	

			Parker Pen Challenge Cup
Fri 2nd Jan 2004	Connacht 0-3 Munster Rugby	Dubarry Park	Celtic League
Sat 10th Jan 2004	Connacht 29-7 Pau	Sportsground	
			Parker Pen Challenge Cup
Sat 17th Jan 2004	Pau 10-6 Connacht	Stade Municipal du Hameau	
			Parker Pen Challenge Cup
Sat 24th Jan 2004	Narbonne 18-27 Connacht	Parc de Sport et de l'Amitie	
			Parker Pen Challenge Cup Quarter-final
Sat 31st Jan 2004	Connacht 16-10 Narbonne	Sportsground	
			Parker Pen Challenge Cup Quarter-final
Sat 7th Feb 2004	Celtic Warriors 40-17 Connacht	Brewery Field	Celtic League
Fri 13th Feb 2004	Edinburgh Rugby 17-32 Connacht	Meadowbank	Celtic League
Sat 21st Feb 2004	Connacht 18-21 Cardiff Blues	Dubarry Park	Celtic League
Sat 28th Feb 2004	Connacht 28-28 Glasgow Rugby	Sportsground	Celtic League
Fri 5th Mar 2004	The Borders 40-29 Connacht	Netherdale	Celtic League
Sat 13th Mar 2004	Connacht 35-24 Leinster Rugby	Sportsground	Celtic League
Fri 26th Mar 2004	Llanelli Scarlets 33-33 Connacht	Stradey Park	Celtic League
Sat 3rd Apr 2004	Connacht 24-21 Ospreys	Sportsground	Celtic League
Sun 11th Apr 2004	NEC Harlequins 31-22 Connacht	The Stoop	
			Parker Pen Challenge Cup Semi-final
Fri 16th Apr 2004	Ulster Rugby 42-27 Connacht	Ravenhill	Celtic League
Sun 25th Apr 2004	Connacht 23-18 NEC Harlequins	Sportsground	
			Parker Pen Challenge Cup Semi-final
Sat 1st May 2004	Connacht 14-32 Newport Gwent Dragons		
		Sportsground	Celtic League
Fri 7th May 2004	Munster Rugby 39-10 Connacht	Thomond Park	Celtic League
Fri 14th May 2004	Connacht 3-20 Celtic Warriors	Sportsground	Celtic League

2004-05

DATE	MATCH	VENUE	COMPETITION
Sat 4th Sept 2004	Connacht 31-15 Glasgow Rugby	Sportsground	Celtic League
Sat 11th Sept 2004	Munster Rugby 27-27 Connacht	Musgrave Park	Celtic League
Sat 18th Sept 2004	Connacht 13-19 Ulster Rugby	Sportsground	Celtic League
Fri 24th Sept 2004	Cardiff Blues 31-6 Connacht	Cardiff Arms Park	Celtic League
Sat 2nd Oct 2004	Connacht 29-27 The Borders	Sportsground	Celtic League
Sat 9th Oct 2004	Llanelli Scarlets 21-29 Connacht	Stradey Park	Celtic League
Sat 16th Oct 2004	Connacht 24-35 Edinburgh Rugby	Sportsground	Celtic League
Sat 23rd Oct 2004	Narbonne 25-11 Connacht	Parc de Sport et de l'Amitie	
			Parker Pen Challenge Cup
Sat 30th Oct 2004	Connacht 40-21 Narbonne	Sportsground	
			Parker Pen Challenge Cup
Fri 5th Nov 2004	Leinster Rugby 18-9 Connacht	Donnybrook	Celtic League
Sun 21st Nov 2004	Ospreys 9-10 Connacht	The Gnoll	Celtic League
Sun 28th Nov 2004	Connacht 19-14 Newport Gwent Dragons		
		Sportsgound	Celtic League
Sat 4th Dec 2004	Connacht 56-3 Montpellier	Sportsgound	
			Parker Pen Challenge Cup
Fri 10th Dec 2004	Montpellier 19-14 Connacht	Stade Sabathé	
			Parker Pen Challenge Cup
Fri 17th Dec 2004	Glasgow Rugby 35-0 Connacht	Hughenden	Celtic League
Mon 27th Dec 2004	Connacht 0-3 Munster Rugby	Sportsground	Celtic League
Sat 1st Jan 2005	Ulster Rugby 23-14 Connacht	Ravenhill	Celtic League
Fri 7th Jan 2005	Grenoble 21-26 Connacht	Stade Lesdiguières	
			Parker Pen Challenge Cup Quarter-final
Sat 15th Jan 2005	Connacht 19-3 Grenoble	Sportsground	
			Parker Pen Challenge Cup Quarter-final
Sat 22nd Jan 2005	Connacht 8-18 Cardiff Blues	Sportsground	Celtic League
Fri 28th Jan 2005	The Borders 9-18 Connacht	Netherdale	Celtic League
Fri 18th Feb 2005	Connacht 11-18 Llanelli Scarlets	Dubarry Park	Celtic League
Fri 4th Mar 2005	Edinburgh Rugby 13-16 Connacht	Murrayfield	Celtic League
Sun 20th Mar 2005	Connacht 21-26 Leinster Rugby	Sportsground	Celtic League
Sat 2nd Apr 2005	Connacht 18-25 Sale Sharks	Sportsground	
			Parker Pen Challenge Cup Semi-final
Sun 10th Apr 2005	Connacht 13-22 Ospreys	Sportsground	Celtic League
Sat 16th Apr 2005	Newport Gwent Dragons 24-19 Connacht		
		Rodney Parade	Celtic League
Sat 24th Apr 2005	Sale Sharks 59-9 Connacht	Edgeley Park	
			Parker Pen Challenge Cup Semi-final

2005-06

DATE	MATCH	VENUE	COMPETITION
Sat 3rd Sept 2005	Connacht 13-9 Cardiff Blues	Sportsground	Celtic League
Sat 10th Sept 2005	Edinburgh Gunners 34-3 Connacht		
		Murrayfield	Celtic League
Sat 17th Sept 2005	Llanelli Scarlets 25-17 Connacht	Racecourse Stadium	Celtic League
Sat 24th Sept 2005	Connacht 15-17 Border Reivers	Sportsground	Celtic League
Sat 1st Oct 2005	Connacht 19-44 Munster Rugby	Sportsground	Celtic League
Fri 7th Oct 2005	Ulster Rugby 36-10 Connacht	Ravenhill	Celtic League
Fri 14th Oct 2005	Ospreys 18-17 Connacht	Liberty Stadium	Celtic League
Sat 22nd Oct 2005	Connacht 62-17 Catania	Sportsground	Challenge Cup
Fri 28th Oct 2005	Montpellier 13-19 Connacht	Stade Sabathé	Challenge Cup
Fri 4th Nov 2005	Glasgow Warriors 30-15 Connacht		
		Hughenden	Celtic League
Sat 3rd Dec 2005	Connacht 9-21 Leinster Rugby	Sportsground	Celtic League
Sat 10th Dec 2005	Worcester Warriors 30-20 Connacht		
		Sixways Stadium	Challenge Cup
Sat 17th Dec 2005	Connacht 22-21 Worcester Warriors		
		Sportsground	Challenge Cup
Tues 27th Dec 2005	Munster Rugby 36-17 Connacht	Thomond Park	Celtic League
Sat 31st Dec 2005	Connacht 22-12 Ulster Rugby	Sportsground	Celtic League
Fri 6th Jan 2006	Newport Gwent Dragons 27-19 Connacht		
		Rodney Parade	Celtic League
Sat 14th Jan 2006	Connacht 43-10 Montpellier	Sportsground	Challenge Cup
Fri 20th Jan 2006	Catania 28-24 Connacht	Santa Maria Goretti	Challenge Cup
Sat 18th Feb 2006	Connacht 33-19 Llanelli Scarlets	Sportsground	Celtic League
Sun 5th Mar 2006	Leinster Rugby 16-13 Connacht	Donnybrook	Celtic League
Fri 24th Mar 2006	Border Reivers 9-11 Connacht	Netherdale	Celtic League
Fri 31st Mar 2006	Newcastle Falcons 23-3 Connacht		
		Kingston Park Stadium	
			Challenge Cup Quarter-final
Sat 15th Apr 2006	Connacht 15-10 Newport Gwent Dragons		
		Sportsground	Celtic League
Sat 29th Apr 2006	Cardiff Blues 30-12 Connacht	Cardiff Arms Park	Celtic League
Fri 5th May 2006	Connacht 16-22 Edinburgh Gunners		
		Sportsground	Celtic League
Fri 12th May 2006	Connacht 16-44 Ospreys	Sportsground	Celtic League
Fri 26th May 2006	Connacht 33-7 Glasgow Warriors	Sportsground	Celtic League

2006-07

DATE	MATCH	VENUE	COMPETITION
Fri 1st Sept 2006	Border Reivers 15-29 Connacht	Netherdale	Magners League
Fri 8th Sept 2006	Connacht 15-10 Ospreys	Sportsground	Magners League
Fri 15th Sept 2006	Connacht 15-37 Llanelli Scarlets	Sportsground	Magners League
Fri 22nd Sept 2006	Connacht 22-22 Edinburgh Rugby	Sportsground	Magners League
Fri 29th Sept 2006	Connacht 16-31 Leinster Rugby	Sportsground	Magners League
Fri 6th Oct 2006	Connacht 17-24 Ulster Rugby	Sportsground	Magners League
Fri 13th Oct 2006	Connacht 16-9 Newport Gwent Dragons		
		Sportsground	Magners League
Fri 20th Oct 2006	Connacht 18-19 NEC Harlequins	Sportsground	Challenge Cup
Sat 28th Oct 2006	Bath Rugby 21-19 Connacht	The Recreation Ground	Challenge Cup
Fri 3rd Nov 2006	Glasgow Warriors 39-34 Connacht		
		Hughenden	Magners League
Sat 18th Nov 2006	Cardiff Blues 15-13 Connacht	Cardiff Arms Park	Magners League
Sun 3rd Dec 2006	Munster Rugby 13-0 Connacht	Thomond Park	Magners League
Fri 8th Dec 2006	Connacht 26-13 Montpellier	Sportsground	Challenge Cup
Fri 15th Dec 2006	Montpellier 35-22 Connacht	Stade Sabathe	Challenge Cup
Tues 26th Dec 2006	Ulster Rugby 20-10 Connacht	Ravenhill	Magners League
Sun 31st Dec 2006	Connacht 28-14 Munster Rugby	Sportsground	Magners League
Fri 12th Jan 2007	Connacht 24-36 Bath Rugby	Sportsground	Challenge Cup
Sat 20th Jan 2007	NEC Harlequins 26-10 Connacht	The Stoop	Challenge Cup
Fri 26th Jan 2007	Edinburgh Rugby 49-31 Connacht	Murrayfield	Magners League
Sat 17th Feb 2007	Ospreys 31-10 Connacht	Liberty Stadium	Magners League
Fri 2nd Mar 2007	Connacht 20-17 Border Reivers	Sportsground	Magners League
Sat 24th Mar 2007	Leinster Rugby 30-21 Connacht	Donnybrook	Magners League
Sat 7th Apr 2007	Connacht 16-16 Cardiff Blues	Sportsground	Magners League

Fri 13th Apr 2007	Connacht 23-40 Glasgow Warriors		
Fri 4th May 2007		Sportsground	Magners League
	Newport Gwent Dragons 23-0 Connacht		
		Rodney Parade	Magners League
Fri 11th May 2007	Llanelli Scarlets 34-11 Connacht	Stradey Park	Magners League

2007-08

DATE	MATCH	VENUE	COMPETITION
Fri 21st Sept 2007	Connacht 22-7 Newport Gwent Dragons		
		Sportsground	Magners League
Fri 28th Sept 2007	Llanellis Scarlets 34-11 Connacht	Stradey Park	Magners League
Fri 5th Oct 2007	Glasgow Warriors 16-15 Connacht		
		Firhill Stadium	Magners League
Fri 12th Oct 2007	Cardiff Blues 30-16 Connacht	Cardiff Arms Park	Magners League
Fri 26th Oct 2007	Connacht 14-14 Edinburgh Rugby	Sportsground	Magners League
Fri 2nd Nov 2007	Leinster Rugby 29-9 Connacht	RDS	Magners League
Fri 9th Nov 2007	Brive 15-6 Connacht	Stade Municipal, Brive	
			Challenge Cup
Fri 16th Nov 2007	Connacht 75-8 El Salvador	Sportsground	Challenge Cup
Fri 23rd Nov 2007	Connacht 13-30 Ulster Rugby	Sportsground	Magners League
Fri 30th Nov 2007	Connacht 10-6 Glasgow Warriors	Sportsground	Magners League
Fri 7th Dec 2007	Connacht 16-13 Newcastle Falcons		
		Sportsground	Challenge Cup
Fri 16th Dec 2007	Newcastle Falcons 39-0 Connacht		
		Kingston Park Stadium	Challenge Cup
Thurs 27th Dec 2007	Munster Rugby 17-0 Connacht	Musgrave Park	Magners League
Fri 4th Jan 2008	Connacht 20-18 Llanelli Scarlets	Sportsground	Magners League
Sun 13th Jan 2008	EL Salvador 0-60 Connacht	Campo de Pepe Rojo	Challenge Cup
Fri 18th Jan 2008	Connacht 15-22 Brive	Sportsground	Challenge Cup
Sat 16th Feb 2008	Ospreys 37-7 Connacht	Liberty Stadium	Magners League
Fri 29th Feb 2008	Connacht 10-16 Leinster Rugby	Sportsground	Magners League
Fri 21st Mar 2008	Edinburgh Rugby 38-8 Connacht	Murrayfield	Magners League
Fri 28th Mar 2008	Connacht 5-16 Munster Rugby	Sportsground	Magners League
Fri 11th Apr 2008	Ulster Rugby 18-6 Connacht	Ravenhill	Magners League
Fri 18th Apr 2008	Newport Gwent Dragons 11-13 Connacht		
		Rodney Parade	Magners League
Fri 2nd May 2008	Connacht 11-39 Cardiff Blues	Sportsground	Magners League
Fri 9th May 2008	Connacht 24-20 Ospreys	Sportsground	Magners League

2008-09

DATE	MATCH	VENUE	COMPETITION
Fri 5th Sept 2008	Connacht 3-16 Ospreys	Sportsground	Magners League
Sat 13th Sept 2008	Scarlets 45-3 Connacht	Stradey Park	Magners League
Fri 19th Sept 2008	Connacht 15-8 Glasgow Warriors	Sportsground	Magners League
Fri 26th Sept 2008	Cardiff Blues 58-0 Connacht	Cardiff Arms Park	Magners League
Sun 5th Oct 2008	Connacht 19-18 Leinster Rugby	Sportsground	Magners League
Fri 10th Oct 2008	Dax 12-30 Connacht	Stade Maurice Boyau	Challenge Cup
Fri 17th Oct 2008	Connacht 10-27 London Irish	Sportsground	Challenge Cup
Fri 24th Oct 2008	Connacht 14-27 Edinburgh Rugby	Sportsground	Magners League
Fri 28th Nov 2008	Ulster Rugby 53-13 Connacht	Ravenhill	Magners League
Sat 6th Dec 2008	Rugby Rovigo 20-35 Connacht	Stadio Mario Battaglini	
			Challenge Cup
Fri 12th Dec 2008	Connacht 30-3 Rugby Rovigo	Sportsground	Challenge Cup
Sun 28th Dec 2008	Connacht 12-6 Munster Rugby	Sportsground	Magners League
Fri 2nd Jan 2009	Leinster Rugby 26-18 Connacht	RDS	Magners League
Fri 9th Jan 2009	Connacht 14-17 Scarlets	Sportsground	Magners League
Sat 17th Jan 2009	London Irish 75-5 Connacht	Madejski Stadium	Challenge Cup
Fri 23rd Jan 2009	Connacht 49-3 Dax	Sportsground	Challenge Cup
Sun 22nd Feb 2009	Ospreys 22-10 Connacht	Liberty Stadium	Magners League
Fri 6th Mar 2009	Connacht 14-19 Cardiff Blues	Sportsground	Magners League
Fri 27th Mar 2009	Edinburgh Rugby 32-5 Connacht	Murrayfield	Magners League
Fri 3rd Apr 2009	Connacht 39-17 Newport Gwent Dragons		
		Sportsground	Magners League
Sat 11th Apr 2009	Northampton Saints 42-13 Connacht		
		Fanklin's Gardens	
			Challenge Cup Quarter-final
Sat 18th Apr 2009	Munster Rugby 25-10 Connacht	Thomond Park	Magners League

Sun 26th Apr 2009	Newport Gwent Dragons 27-14 Connacht		
Fri 8th May 2009		Rodney Parade	Magners League
	Connacht 12-14 Ulster Rugby	Sportsground	Magners League
Fri 15th May 2009	Glasgow Warriors 30-9 Connacht	Firhill Stadium	Magners League

2009-10

DATE	MATCH	VENUE	COMPETITION
Fri 4th Sept 2009	Connacht 12-19 Ospreys	Sportsground	Magners League
Fri 11th Sept 2009	Edinburgh Rugby 62-13 Connacht		
		Murrayfield	Magners League
Fri 18th Sept 2009	Connacht 18-16 Cardiff Blues	Sportsground	Magners League
Fri 25th Sept 2009	Connacht 6-30 Ulster Rugby	Sportsground	Magners League
Sat 3rd Oct 2009	Newport Gwent Dragons 23-10 Connacht		
		Rodney Parade	Magners League
Fri 9th Oct 2009	Connacht 46-6 Olympus Rugby XV Madrid		
		Sportsground	Amlin Challenge Cup
Fri 16th Oct 2009	Montpellier 19-22 Connacht	Stade Yves du Manoir, Montpellier	
			Amlin Challenge Cup
Fri 23rd Oct 2009	Glasgow Warriors 34-20 Connacht		
		Firhill Stadium	Magners League
Fri 30th Oct 2009	Connacht 16-10 Scarlets	Sportsground	Magners League
Sun 6th Dec 2009	Cardiff Blues 21-9 Connacht	Cardiff City Stadium	
			Magners League
Sat 12th Dec 2009	Worcester Warriors 21-26 Connacht		
		Sixways Stadium	
			Amlin Challenge Cup
Fri 18th Dec 2009	Connacht 19-7 Worcester Warriors		
		Sportsground	
			Amlin Challenge Cup
Sat 26th Dec 2009	Munster Rugby 35-3 Connacht	Thomond Park	Magners League
Fri 15th Jan 2010	Connacht 20-10 Montpellier	Sportsground	Amlin Challenge Cup
Sat 23rd Jan 2010	Olympus Rugby XV Madrid 0-66 Connacht		
		Ciuadad Universitaria	
			Amlin Challenge Cup
Sun 21st Feb 2010	Ospreys 19-17 Connacht	Liberty Stadium	Magners League
Fri 5th Mar 2010	Connacht 19-19 Glasgow Warriors		
		Sportsground	Magners League
Wed 17th Mar 2010	Connacht 16-3 Newport Gwent Dragons		
		Sportsground	Magners League
Sat 27th Mar 2010	Leinster Rugby 17-14 Connacht	RDS	Magners League
Fri 2nd Apr 2010	Connacht 22-21 Edinburgh Rugby	Sportsground	Magners League
Sat 10th Apr 2010	Connacht 23-20 Bourgoin	Sportsground	
			Amlin Challenge Cup Quarter-final
Sun 18th Apr 2010	Connacht 12-18 Munster Rugby	Sportsground	Magners League
Wed 21st Apr 2010	Connacht 27-13 Leinster Rugby	Sportsground	Magners League
Sun 25th Apr 2010	Scarlets 58-10 Connacht	Parc y Scarlets	Magners League
Fri 30th Apr 2010	Connacht 12-19 Toulon	Sportsground	
			Amlin Challenge Cup Semi-final
Fri 7th May 2010	Ulster Rugby 41-10 Connacht	Ravenhill	Magners League

2010-11

DATE	MATCH	VENUE	COMPETITION
Sat 4th Sept 2010	Connacht 40-17 Newport Gwent Dragons		
		Sportsground	Magners League
Sat 11th Sept 2010	Scarlets 35-33 Connacht	Parc y Scarlets	Magners League
Fri 17th Sept 2010	Glasgow Warriors 17-19 Connacht		
		Firhill Stadium	Magners League
Sat 25th Sept 2010	Connacht 15-15 Ulster Rugby	Sportsground	Magners League
Thurs 30th Sept 2010	Cardiff Blues 22-6 Connacht	Cardiff City Stadium	Magners League
Sat 9th Oct 2010	I Cavalieri Estra 23-21 Connacht	Stade Lungobisenzio	
			Amlin Challenge Cup
Fri 15th Oct 2010	Connacht 16-13 Bayonne	Sportsground	Amlin Challenge Cup
Sat 23rd Oct 2010	Connacht 6-18 Leinster Rugby	Sportsground	Magners League
Sat 30th Oct 2010	Benetton Treviso 24-17 Connacht	Stadio di Monigo	Magners League
Fri 19th Nov 2010	Connacht 15-16 Ospreys	Sportsground	Magners League
Fri 26th Nov 2010	Edinburgh Rugby 24-19 Connacht	Murrayfield	Magners League
Sun 12th Dec 2010	Harlequins 20-9 Connacht	The Stoop	Amlin Challenge Cup

DATE	MATCH	VENUE	COMPETITION
Fri 17th Dec 2010	Connacht 9-15 Harlequins	Sportsground	Amlin Challenge Cup
Mon 27th Dec 2010	Connacht 12-16 Munster Rugby	Sportsground	Magners League
Sat 1st Jan 2011	Leinster Rugby 30-8 Connacht	RDS	Magners League
Thurs 6th Jan 2011	Newport Gwent Dragons 17-16 Connacht	Rodney Parade	Magners League
Sat 15th Jan 2011	Bayonne 21-35 Connacht	Stade Jean Dauger	Amlin Challenge Cup
Sat 22nd Jan 2011	Connacht 83-7 I Cavalieri Estra	Sportsground	Amlin Challenge Cup
Sat 12th Feb 2011	Connacht 17-13 Scarlets	Sportsground	Magners League
Fri 18th Feb 2011	Connacht 37-8 Glasgow Warriors	Sportsground	Magners League
Sun 27th Feb 2011	Ospreys 33-18 Connacht	Liberty Stadium	Magners League
Fri 4th Mar 2011	Connacht 31-25 Benetton Treviso	Sportsground	Magners League
Fri 11th Mar 2011	Connacht 11-6 Aironi Rugby	Sportsground	Magners League
Sat 26th Mar 2011	Aironi Rugby 25-13 Connacht	Stadio Zaffanella	Magners League
Fri 1st Apr 2011	Connacht 27-23 Edinburgh Rugby	Sportsground	Magners League
Fri 15th Apr 2011	Connacht 12-26 Cardiff Blues	Sportsground	Magners League
Fri 22nd Apr 2011	Ulster Rugby 27-16 Connacht	Ravenhill	Magners League
Fri 6th May 2011	Munster Rugby 22-6 Connacht	Thomond Park	Magners League

2011-12

DATE	MATCH	VENUE	COMPETITION
Sat 3rd Sept 2011	Benetton Treviso 9-11 Connacht	Stadio di Monigo	RaboDirect PRO12
Sat 10th Sept 2011	Connacht 13-11 Scarlets	Sportsground	RaboDirect PRO12
Fri 16th Sept 2011	Edinburgh Rugby 19-14 Connacht	Murrayfield	RaboDirect PRO12
Fri 23rd Sept 2011	Connacht 17-13 Newport Gwent Dragons	Sportsground	RaboDirect PRO12
Fri 30th Sept 2011	Ospreys 26-21 Connacht	Liberty Stadium	RaboDirect PRO12
Sat 8th Oct 2011	Leinster Rugby 30-20 Connacht	RDS	RaboDirect PRO12
Sat 29th Oct 2011	Connacht 20-26 Cardiff Blues	Sportsground	RaboDirect PRO12
Sat 5th Nov 2011	Ulster Rugby 22-3 Connacht	Ravenhill	RaboDirect PRO12
Fri 11th Nov 2011	Harlequins 25-17 Connacht	The Stoop	Heineken Cup
Sat 19th Nov 2011	Connacht 10-36 Toulouse	Sportsground	Heineken Cup
Sat 26th Nov 2011	Connacht 6-17 Ospreys	Sportsground	RaboDirect PRO12
Fri 2nd Dec 2011	Connacht 13-15 Benetton Treviso	Sportsground	RaboDirect PRO12
Sat 10th Dec 2011	Connacht 10-14 Gloucester Rugby	Sportsground	Heineken Cup
Sat 17th Dec 2011	Gloucester Rugby 23-19 Connacht	Kingsholm	Heineken Cup
Mon 26th Dec 2011	Munster Rugby 24-9 Connacht	Thomond Park	RaboDirect PRO12
Sun 1st Jan 2012	Connacht 13-15 Leinster Rugby	Sportsground	RaboDirect PRO12
Sat 7th Jan 2012	Aironi Rugby 20-6 Connacht	Stadio Zaffanella	RaboDirect PRO12
Sat 14th Jan 2012	Toulouse 24-3 Connacht	Stade Ernest Wallon	Heineken Cup
Fri 20th Jan 2012	Connacht 9-8 Harlequins	Sportsground	Heineken Cup
Fri 10th Feb 2012	Cardiff Blues 22-15 Connacht	Cardiff Arms Park	RaboDirect PRO12
Sat 18th Feb 2012	Connacht 13-13 Glasgow Warriors	Sportsground	RaboDirect PRO12
Fri 24th Feb 2012	Connacht 26-13 Edinburgh Rugby	Sportsground	RaboDirect PRO12
Fri 2nd Mar 2012	Scarlets 38-10 Connacht	Parc y Scarlets	RaboDirect PRO12
Sat 24th Mar 2012	Connacht 16-20 Munster Rugby	Sportsground	RaboDirect PRO12
Fri 30th Mar 2012	Newport Gwent Dragons 19-27 Connacht	Rodney Parade	RaboDirect PRO12
Sat 14th Apr 2012	Connacht 26-21 Ulster Rugby	Sportsground	RaboDirect PRO12
Sat 21st Apr 2012	Connacht 19-16 Aironi Rugby	Sportsground	RaboDirect PRO12
Sat 5th May 2012	Glasgow Warriors 24-3 Connacht	Firhill Stadium	RaboDirect PRO12

2012-13

DATE	MATCH	VENUE	COMPETITION
Sat 1st Sept 2012	Connacht 9-13 Cardiff Blues	Sportground	RaboDirect PRO12
Fri 7th Sept 2012	Zebre 17-30 Connacht	Stadio XXV Aprile	RaboDirect PRO12
Sat 15th Sept 2012	Connacht 11-24 Scarlets	Sportsground	RaboDirect PRO12
Fri 21st Sept 2012	Glasgow Warriors 27-17 Connacht	Scotstoun Stadium	RaboDirect PRO12
Fri 28th Sept 2012	Connacht 34-6 Leinster Rugby	Sportsground	RaboDirect PRO12
Fri 5th Oct 2012	Ulster Rugby 25-0 Connacht	Ravenhill	RaboDirect PRO12
Sat 13th Oct 2012	Zebre 10-19 Connacht	Stadio XXV Aprile	Heineken Cup
Sat 20th Oct 2012	Connacht 22-30 Harlequins	Sportsground	Heineken Cup
Sat 27th Oct 2012	Ospreys 26-9 Connacht	Liberty Stadium	RaboDirect PRO12
Sat 3rd Nov 2012	Connacht 18-3 Benetton Treviso	Sportsground	RaboDirect PRO12
Fri 23rd Nov 2012	Newport Gwent Dragons 14-3 Connacht	Rodney Parade	RaboDirect PRO12
Sat 1st Dec 2012	Connacht 23-24 Edinburgh Rugby	Sportsground	RaboDirect PRO12
Fri 7th Dec 2012	Connacht 22-14 Biarritz Olympique Pays Basque	Sportsground	Heineken Cup
Fri 14th Dec 2012	Biarritz Olympique Pays Basque 17-0 Connacht	Parc des Sports Aguilera	Heineken Cup
Sat 22nd Dec 2012	Connacht 12-16 Munster Rugby	Sportsground	RaboDirect PRO12
Sat 29th Dec 2012	Leinster Rugby 17-0 Connacht	RDS	RaboDirect PRO12
Sat 5th Jan 2013	Connacht 30-11 Newport Gwent Dragons	Sportsground	RaboDirect PRO12
Sat 12th Jan 2013	Harlequins 47-8 Connacht	The Stoop	Heineken Cup
Fri 18th Jan 2013	Connacht 25-20 Zebre	Sportsground	Heineken Cup
Fri 8th Feb 2013	Scarlets 25-15 Connacht	Parc y Scarlets	RaboDirect PRO12
Fri 15th Feb 2013	Connacht 22-10 Ospreys	Sportsground	RaboDirect PRO12
Fri 22nd Feb 2013	Cardiff Blues 22-26 Connacht	Cardiff Arms Park	RaboDirect PRO12
Fri 1st Mar 2013	Connacht 23-19 Zebre	Sportsground	RaboDirect PRO12
Sat 23rd Mar 2013	Munster Rugby 22-0 Connacht	Musgrave Park	RaboDirect PRO12
Fri 12th Apr 2013	Edinburgh Rugby 24-32 Connacht	Murrayfield	RaboDirect PRO12
Fri 19th Apr 2013	Connacht 18-34 Ulster Rugby	Sportsground	RaboDirect PRO12
Fri 26th Apr 2013	Benetton Treviso 23-23 Connacht	Stadio di Monigo	RaboDirect PRO12
Fri 3rd May 2013	Connacht 3-20 Glasgow Warriors	Sportsground	RaboDirect PRO12

2013-14

DATE	MATCH	VENUE	COMPETITION
Sat 7th Sept 2013	Connacht 25-16 Zebre	Sportsground	RaboDirect PRO12
Fri 13th Sept 2013	Cardiff Blues 21-10 Connacht	Arms Park	RaboDirect PRO12
Sat 21st Sept 2013	Connacht 7-18 Ulster Rugby	Sportsground	RaboDirect PRO12
Sat 28th Sept 2013	Connacht 26-43 Ospreys	Sportsground	RaboDirect PRO12
Fri 4th Oct 2013	Benetton Treviso 23-3 Connacht	Stadio Monigo	RaboDirect PRO12
Fri 11th Oct 2013	Connacht 17-23 Saracens	Sportsground	Heineken Cup
Sat 19th Oct 2013	Zebre 6-33 Connacht	Stadio XXV Aprile	Heineken Cup
Sat 26th Oct 2013	Leinster Rugby 16-13 Connacht	RDS	RaboDirect PRO12
Sat 2nd Nov 2013	Connacht 12-19 Glasgow Warriors	Sportsground	RaboDirect PRO12
Sat 23rd Nov 2013	Connacht 21-24 Scarlets	Sportsground	RaboDirect PRO12
Fri 29th Nov 2013	Edinburgh Rugby 43-10 Connacht	Murrayfield	RaboDirect PRO12
Sun 8th Dec 2013	Toulouse 14-16 Connacht	Stade Ernest-Wallon	Heineken Cup
Sat 14th Dec 2013	Connacht 9-37 Toulouse	Sportsground	Heineken Cup
Sat 21st Dec 2013	Connacht 14-11 Newport Gwent Dragons	Sportsground	RaboDirect PRO12
Fri 27th Dec 2013	Munster Rugby 22-16 Connacht	Thomond Park	RaboDirect PRO12
Sat 4th Jan 2014	Connacht 8-16 Leinster Rugby	Sportsground	RaboDirect PRO12
Sat 11th Jan 2014	Connacht 20-3 Zebre	Sportsground	Heineken Cup
Sat 18th Jan 2014	Saracens 64-6 Connacht	Allianz Park	Heineken Cup
Sat 9th Feb 2014	Glasgow Warriors 8-6 Connacht	Scotstoun Stadium	RaboDirect PRO12
Sat 15th Feb 2014	Connacht 11-7 Edinburgh Rugby	Sportsground	RaboDirect PRO12
Sun 23rd Feb 2014	Zebre 19-27 Connacht	Stadio XXV Aprile	RaboDirect PRO12
Sat 1st Mar 2014	Connacht 38-6 Benetton Treviso	Sportsground	RaboDirect PRO12
Sun 23rd Mar 2014	Newport Gwent Dragons 8-24 Connacht	Rodney Parade	RaboDirect PRO12
Sun 30th Mar 2014	Scarlets 32-30 Connacht	Parc y Scarlets	RaboDirect PRO12
Fri 11th Apr 2014	Ulster Rugby 58-12 Connacht	Ravenhill Stadium	RaboDirect PRO12
Sat 19th Apr 2014	Connacht 23-32 Munster Rugby	Sportsground	RaboDirect PRO12
Sat 3rd May 2014	Connacht 15-22 Cardiff Blues	Sportsground	RaboDirect PRO12
Sat 10th May 2014	Ospreys 45-20 Connacht	Liberty Stadium	RaboDirect PRO12

2014-15

DATE	MATCH	VENUE	COMPETITION
Sat 6th Sept 2014	Connacht 16-11 Newport Gwent Dragons	Sportsground	GUINNESS PRO12
Fri 12th Sept 2014	Edinburgh Rugby 13-14 Connacht	BT Murrayfield	GUINNESS PRO12
Fri 19th Sept 2014	Connacht 10-9 Leinster Rugby	Sportsground	GUINNESS PRO12
Fri 26th Sept 2014	Glasgow Warriors 39-21 Connacht	Scotstoun Stadium	GUINNESS PRO12

Fri 3rd Oct 2014	Connacht 24-24 Cardiff Blues	Sportsground	GUINNESS PRO12
Fri 10th Oct 2014	Benetton Treviso 6-9 Connacht	Stadio Monigo	GUINNESS PRO12
Sat 18th Oct 2014	Connacht 48-12 La Rochelle	Sportsground	
		European Rugby Challenge Cup	
Sat 25th Oct 2014	Exeter Chiefs 33-13 Connacht	Sandy Park Stadium	
		European Rugby Challenge Cup	
Fri 31st Oct 2014	Ospreys 26-11 Connacht	Liberty Stadium	GUINNESS PRO12
Fri 21st Nov 2014	Connacht 43-3 Zebre	Sportsground	GUINNESS PRO12
Sat 29th Nov 2014	Connacht 14-8 Scarlets	Sportsground	GUINNESS PRO12
Sat 6th Dec 2014	Connacht 42-19 Bayonne	Sportsground	
		European Rugby Challenge Cup	
Sat 13th Dec 2014	Bayonne 27-29 Connacht	Stade Jean-Dauger	
		European Rugby Challenge Cup	
Fri 19th Dec 2014	Leinster Rugby 21-11 Connacht	RDS Arena	GUINNESS PRO12
Fri 26th Dec 2014	Ulster Rugby 13-10 Connacht	Kingspan Stadium	GUINNESS PRO12
Thurs 1st Jan 2015	Connacht 24-16 Munster Rugby	Sportsground	GUINNESS PRO12
Fri 9th Jan 2015	Connacht 13-16 Edinburgh Rugby	Sportsground	GUINNESS PRO12
Sun 18th Jan 2015	Connacht 24-33 Exeter Chiefs	Sportsground	
		European Rugby Challenge Cup	
Sat 24th Jan 2015	La Rochelle 20-30 Connacht	Stade Marcel Deflandre	
		European Rugby Challenge Cup	
Sun 15th Feb 2015	Scarlets 32-14 Connacht	Parc y Scarlets	GUINNESS PRO12
Sun 22nd Feb 2015	Newport Gwent Dragons 25-30 Connacht		
		Rodney Parade	GUINNESS PRO12
Sun 1st Mar 2015	Connacht 53-5 Benetton Treviso	Sportsground	GUINNESS PRO12
Fri 6th Mar 2015	Cardiff Blues 18-17 Connacht	BT Sport Cardiff Arms Park	
			GUINNESS PRO12
Sat 28th Mar 2015	Munster Rugby 42-20 Connacht	Thomond Park	GUINNESS PRO12
Fri 3rd Apr 2015	Gloucester Rugby 14-7 Connacht	Kingsholm Stadium	
		European Rugby Challenge Cup Quarter-final	
Sat 11th Apr 2015	Connacht 20-27 Ulster Rugby	Sportsground	GUINNESS PRO12
Sat 25th Apr 2015	Connacht 13-31 Glasgow Warriors		
		Sportsground	GUINNESS PRO12
Sat 9th May 2015	Zebre 10-40 Connacht	Stadio Sergio Lanfranchi	
			GUINNESS PRO12
Sat 16th May 2015	Connacht 20-24 Ospreys	Sportsground	GUINNESS PRO12
Sun 24th May	Gloucester 40-32 Connacht	Kingsholm Stadium	
		Champions Cup play-off	

◼ 2015-16

DATE	MATCH	VENUE	COMPETITION
Fri 4th Sept 2015	Connacht 29-23 Newport Gwent Dragons		
		Sportsground	GUINNESS PRO12
Fri 11th Sept 2015	Glasgow Warriors 33-32 Connacht		
		Scotstoun Stadium	GUINNESS PRO12

Sat 3rd Oct 2015	Connacht 36-31 Cardiff Blues	Sportsground	GUINNESS PRO12
Fri 16th Oct 2015	Connacht 34-15 Zebre Rugby	Sportsground	GUINNESS PRO12
Sat 24th Oct 2015	Ospreys 16-21 Connacht	Liberty Stadium	GUINNESS PRO12
Sat 31st Oct 2015	Connacht 14-9 Edinburgh Rugby	Sportsground	GUINNESS PRO12
Fri 6th Nov 2015	Connacht 33-19 Benetton Rugby Treviso		
		Sportsground	GUINNESS PRO12
Sat 14th Nov 2015	Enisei-STM 14-31 Connacht	Central Stadium	
		European Rugby Challenge Cup	
Sat 21st Nov 2015	Connacht 21-17 Brive	Sportsground	
		European Rugby Challenge Cup	
Sat 28th Nov 2015	Munster Rugby 12-18 Connacht	Thomond Park	GUINNESS PRO12
Fri 4th Dec 2015	Cardiff Blues 20-16 Connacht	BT Sport Cardiff Arms Park	
			GUINNESS PRO12
Fri 11th Dec 2015	Connacht 25-10 Newcastle Falcons		
		Sportsground	
		European Rugby Challenge Cup	
Sun 20th Dec 2015	Newcastle Falcons 29-5 Connacht	Kingston Park	
		European Rugby Challenge Cup	
Sat 26th Dec 2015	Connacht 3-10 Ulster Rugby	Sportsground	GUINNESS PRO12
Fri 1st Jan 2016	Leinster Rugby 13-0 Connacht	RDS Arena	GUINNESS PRO12
Sun 10th Jan 2016	Scarlets 21-19 Connacht	Parc y Scarlets	GUINNESS PRO12
Sat 16th Jan 2016	Brive 21-18 Connacht	Stade Amedee-Domenech	
		European Rugby Challenge Cup	
Sat 23rd Jan 2016	Connacht 47-5 Enisei-STM	Sportsground	
		European Rugby Challenge Cup	
Sat 30th Jan 2016	Connacht 30-17 Scarlets	Sportsground	GUINNESS PRO12
Thur 11th Feb 2016	Newport Gwent Dragons 21-16 Connacht		
		Rodney Parade	GUINNESS PRO12
Sat 20th Feb 2016	Zebre 34-51 Connacht	Stadio Sergio Lanfranchi	
			GUINNESS PRO12
Sat 27th Feb 2016	Connacht 30-22 Ospreys	Sportsground	GUINNESS PRO12
Fri 4th Mar 2016	Edinburgh Rugby 23-28 Connacht	BT Murrayfield	GUINNESS PRO12
Sat 26th Mar 2016	Connacht 7-6 Leinster Rugby	Sportsground	GUINNESS PRO12
Fri 1st Apr 2016	Ulster Rugby 18-10 Connacht	Kingspan Stadium	GUINNESS PRO12
Sat 9th Apr 2016	Grenoble 33-32 Connacht	Stade des Alpes	
		European Rugby Challenge Cup Quarter-final	
Sat 16th Apr 2016	Connacht 35-14 Munster Rugby	Sportsground	GUINNESS PRO12
Fri 29th Apr 2016	Benetton Rugby Treviso 22-21 Connacht		
		Stadio Monigo	GUINNESS PRO12
Sat 7th May 2016	Connacht 14-7 Glasgow Warriors	Sportsground	GUINNESS PRO12
Sat 21st May 2016	Connacht 16-11 Glasgow Warriors		
		Sportsground	
			GUINNESS PRO12 Play off
Sat 28th May 2016	Connacht 20-10 Leinster Rugby	BT Murrayfield	
			GUINNESS PRO12 Final